Early praise for
101 Design Ingredients to Solve Big Tech Problems

Startup founders and enterprise agilists should keep their copies of *101 Design Ingredients* nearby! Full of great insight and suggestions, the book guides teams through common scenarios—recipes—ensuring teams have the best chance of success.

> **Nicholas Muldoon**
> Agile evangelist at Twitter

The same mistakes are often repeated in technology projects. It is easy to develop blind spots or simply get stuck. Often, all we need is a simple yet powerful ingredient to get us back on track. Eewei's book is chock-full of such ingredients—easily digestible and packed with wisdom.

> **Paul Golding**
> Chief alpha maestro, AlphaPunk; chief scientist, Art.com

An excellent, practical guide that will help tech entrepreneurs solve the significant challenges that come along with growing a startup. Packed with clever and insightful illustrations, this little recipe book will help entrepreneurs avoid common mistakes and solve big challenges.

> **Dave Gray**
> Entrepreneur, founder of XPLANE, and author of
> *The Connected Company* and *Gamestorming*

In life, the trick is to find a balance between simplicity and clarity of thought and the complexity of the real world. Eewei describes a host of simple ingredients and combines them in recipes in just the right proportions. Beautifully presented, sharply written, and valuable to experts and newcomers alike.

➤ **Giles Colborne**
   Author of *Simple and Usable*

101 Design Ingredients will help you look at the world differently while sharing wisdom and insight into how some of the world's greatest leaders and organizations are doing it.

➤ **Jonathan Rasmusson**
   Author of *The Agile Samurai*

101 Design Ingredients to Solve Big Tech Problems

Eewei Chen

with illustrations by Robert André

The Pragmatic Bookshelf

Dallas, Texas • Raleigh, North Carolina

Many of the designations used by manufacturers and sellers to distinguish their products are claimed as trademarks. Where those designations appear in this book, and The Pragmatic Programmers, LLC was aware of a trademark claim, the designations have been printed in initial capital letters or in all capitals. The Pragmatic Starter Kit, The Pragmatic Programmer, Pragmatic Programming, Pragmatic Bookshelf, PragProg and the linking *g* device are trademarks of The Pragmatic Programmers, LLC.

Every precaution was taken in the preparation of this book. However, the publisher assumes no responsibility for errors or omissions, or for damages that may result from the use of information (including program listings) contained herein.

Our Pragmatic courses, workshops, and other products can help you and your team create better software and have more fun. For more information, as well as the latest Pragmatic titles, please visit us at *http://pragprog.com*.

The team that produced this book includes:

Jacquelyn Carter (editor)

Potomac Indexing, LLC (indexer)

Candace Cunningham (copyeditor)

David J Kelly (typesetter)

Janet Furlow (producer)

Juliet Benda (rights)

Ellie Callahan (support)

Printed in the United States of America.
ISBN-13: 978-1-937785-32-1
Printed on acid-free paper.
Book version: P1.0—July, 2013

This book is dedicated to the memory of our beloved son Joseph Christopher Chen, who had the most perfect heart.

March 7–April 14, 1997

Contents

Part III — Ingredients to Help You Cross the Finish Line

Part IV — Ingredients to Get More of What You Want

Part V — Recipes for Success

Foreword

As individuals in organizations, our daily lives are filled with ideas to turn into reality, myriad problems to be solved, lists of core business needs to be fulfilled, and many team and people challenges to be overcome. Regardless of the size of your organization, your position within it, the nature of your product or service, or the impact you have on the world, you play an important part in solving big problems and creating amazing and innovative products and services.

As a leader, I value simplicity. The success with which I can make good decisions, decouple difficult dependencies, and give good guidance to my team tends to improve in direct proportion to how simply I can articulate the problems and the outcomes I would like to achieve. This clarity is needed at all levels, whether you are steering a company, leading a team, or contributing to a project as an individual.

So how do you take on these big complex challenges while keeping things simple, focused, and clearly articulated? Eewei has written a book that will inspire innovation while helping you manage the complexities of modern business problems. It describes an approach that employs a simple metaphor—one of cooking, using ingredients and recipes to "cook up" success. This approach gives you two very important tools.

Firstly, the book details many tested ingredients from which to build your recipes. Everyone knows that in any recipe, quality ingredients are key. Eewei adds his own secret sauces, giving you 101 broadly applicable and highly valuable ingredients that come from his extensive experience solving significant business problems and creating delightful products and solutions. He includes ingredients that speak to team and motivation, and ingredients that discuss business, feature, and prioritization needs. Most importantly, he includes ingredients that help foster innovative and differentiated thinking.

Secondly, the book gives structure to the act of simplifying complex scenarios. Eewei's approach asks you to create a recipe for a solution, a recipe that breaks down a problem into the multiple ingredients necessary to achieve a successful outcome for the innovation or business problem at hand. You can use this structured approach in a variety of ways. You can use it on your own, perhaps as an aid to deeper thinking. You can use it in a team setting to help brainstorm a problem. Or perhaps you can use it to articulate a direction to a team in a manageable and understandable way. The recipe metaphor feels really natural and easy to use.

Of course, quality ingredients and a good recipe are keys to baking your "solution cake," but that's not all that's needed. The real value comes when you bring your own insights and experiences to the process. Eewei uses some of his ingredients to pull together a number of sample recipes for common situations, using well-known companies as examples. This really helps you to see the possibilities this approach can provide, and will kick-start your thinking as you begin to use recipes to tackle your biggest challenges. By using Eewei's ingredients (and maybe some of your own!) to write a customized recipe for your problem or business aspiration, you can consciously and deliberately move your projects forward based on a clear and concise recipe for success.

Happy baking!

Paul Hammond
Engineering director
Microsoft

Acknowledgments

To Fatima, Joseph, Ethan, and Faith Chen, my amazing wife and children, for your uncompromising love, support, and belief in me and my crazy ideas. This is one that worked!

To my Ma and Dee for allowing me to be a responsible adult every now and again. To my brother Eewen and my sister Eelyn for just being around. I hope you are proud of me and proud that this book exists.

To the team at Pragmatic Bookshelf, Andy Hunt, Dave Thomas, Susannah Pfalzer, and Jackie Carter—especially Jackie for your guidance and constant nagging that helped me fine-tune and get through what has been an amazing journey of self-discovery.

To Jonathan Rasmusson for introducing me to Pragmatic and convincing me to submit my ideas for this book. A big thank-you to all my awesome book reviewers: Jonathan Rasmusson, Paul Hammond, Nicholas Muldoon, Paul Golding, Dave Gray, Giles Colborne, Jez Humble, Cennydd Bowles, Martin Belam, Chloe Barker, Marc McNeill, Adrian Howard, Alison Austin, and Anders Ramsey.

Thank you, everyone. You've all played such a crucial part in the creation, testing, and fine-tuning of this book—a book that would not exist today if you all didn't prod, push, and kick me into action. I am forever grateful.

Introduction

Technology and business teams continue to deliver products and services to solve bigger and bigger real-world issues. It doesn't really matter whether you're in the design, television, music, Internet, publishing, consultancy, software, marketing, finance, healthcare, or some other industry—many of the big problems facing teams today are the same. How do we innovate? How do we work better as a team? What problems are we meant to be solving? How do we keep our customers happy?

101 Design Ingredients is more than a book. It's a lightweight, supereasy-to-digest problem-solving toolset. You'll learn how to apply to your projects insights from leaders in the design-thinking, agile, lean-startup, product, entertainment, and business-strategy worlds. Your team isn't facing anything today that hasn't already been tackled before. This book will help you and your team work together to better understand problems so you can come up with solutions quickly, easily, and confidently.

Let's face it: we could all use a little more time to get things right, but we often don't get it. Sometimes all you need is a quick flash of inspiration to get you through your project. I wrote *101 Design Ingredients* to help you get reinspired. Use it when you need a boost to keep you going. Start from the beginning to kick-start a project, inject some creativity when you're stuck in a rut, or pick up speed near the end to finish strong. It doesn't matter where you are in your project or what problem you're facing—there's always a solution.

You'll never again think twice about tackling problems, and you'll work well together with your team to solve them.

Who This Book Is For

If you've ever worked on a project where changing customer needs, business goals, and market requirements play a vital part in defining success, this book is for you. No matter whether you're a designer, developer, project manager, business stakeholder, startup founder, product owner, business analyst, usability researcher, branding expert, or marketing or sales staff, this book will give you practical advice to challenge and help you work as part of a team to solve problems.

The ingredients and recipes in this book will help you, whether you're a beginner starting out on your first technology project or a seasoned professional who has been tackling the same big problems for years and needs a fresh approach.

How To Read This Book

101 Design Ingredients is a quick-reference guide that tech teams can use to identify and solve problems fast. It's perfect for your morning commute, a quick read before going to bed, or even an elevator ride. The bite-sized ingredients and recipes are easily consumable in short periods of time. Glance down the list of ingredients and apply the useful hints and tips to solve your biggest problems immediately. It's really that easy.

If your team and your business find it hard to just identify the right problems, *101 Design Ingredients* will help you prioritize and then will act as a catalyst, each ingredient providing simple, practical advice you can start using at any point in a project.

The first four sections of the book correspond to the four stages of a project: Ingredients to Get You Started, Ingredients to Keep You Going, Ingredients to Help You Cross the Finish Line, and Ingredients to Get More of What You Want. You can start with the stage of the project that you're in now, or dive straight into any ingredient that strikes your fancy.

In part V you'll see ten real-world case studies of how companies combined the ingredients to create their own recipes for success, and you'll learn how to apply the ingredients to meet your own specific needs in a matter of minutes.

Online Resources

This book is an open invitation for teams and individuals to connect to discuss shared problems. There are many ways to do that.

This book has its own page on the Pragmatic Bookshelf website: http://pragprog.com/titles/ec101di. Feel free to ask me questions about the book, discuss problems, and share case studies on the discussion forum. If you find any mistakes in the book, please report them on the errata page so we can address them as soon as possible.

Additionally, be sure to visit this book's website,[1] to find, create, and share even more ingredients and recipes. Follow us on Twitter at @101DI and on Facebook at 101 Design Ingredients.[2,3]

I hope you enjoy experimenting with the ingredients and solving problems both at work and in your personal life.

Eewei Chen
me@eewei.com
June 2013

---

1. http://www.101DesignIngredients.com
2. https://twitter.com/101DI
3. http://www.facebook.com/pages/101-Design-Ingredients/474373989295633

Part I

Ingredients to Get You Started

Identify the Root Cause

Step back to see why it really isn't working.

"It isn't that they can't see the solution. It is that they can't see the problem."
—Gilbert K. Chesterton, writer

The Problem

Teams constantly fire-fight instead of tackling bigger issues because companies want instant gratification: any result as long as it immediately satisfies stakeholders and customers.

The Solution

Solve the real big issues, and you'll solve related ones too.

- Ask questions. I like asking "five whys."[4] Start with why a specific problem exists and note the main reason. Next ask why this main reason exists. Do this at least four more times, questioning the last main reason each time. The last problem is a possible root cause you should address.

- Prioritize. In most situations there are multiple root causes,[5] so prioritize which ones to tackle based on urgency, size of impact, subsequent problems solved, dependency, and ease of resolution.

- Track improvements. Take note of new problems that arise and any that persist. Add these to an up-to-date list so you don't lose track of them. Identify related issues and group those together. Put measures in place to prevent problems from occurring again.[6]

---

4. http://www.bulsuk.com/2009/03/5-why-finding-root-causes.html
5. http://www.kitchensoap.com/2012/02/10/each-necessary-but-only-jointly-sufficient/
6. http://www.kitchensoap.com/2012/09/21/a-mature-role-for-automation-part-i/

Ingredient 2

Understand Customer Needs

Give them what they really want.

"People's behavior makes sense if you think about it in terms of their goals, needs, and motives."
—Thomas Mann, writer, critic, and Nobel Prize laureate

The Problem

Customers leave when there's nothing special to keep them loyal to a brand's product or service.

The Solution

Target a customer's deepest desires and solve problems that really annoy them.

- Get real. Gain firsthand experience of what customers actually do and feel. Martin Belam, from *The Guardian* newspaper, conducted guerrilla usability testing in public places to better understand customer needs in a natural environment.[7]

- Identify barriers. Find out what's stopping customers from completing important tasks. Create situations more conducive to success. I refer to cognitive models like BJ Fogg's behavior model, which shows it is possible to motivate and train people to overcome barriers using well-timed "triggers" to increase their likelihood of success.[8]

- Co-design.[9] I've worked with customers to visualize better solutions to a problem together. Don't take their suggestions too literally, though, because most of the time they won't know what they mean until you show it to them.

7.   http://www.currybet.net/cbet_blog/2011/06/changing-guardian-guerilla-usability-testing.php

8.   http://www.behaviormodel.org/

9.   http://www.designcouncil.org.uk/resources-and-events/design-ers/design-glossary/co-design/

Ingredient 3

Promote Your Team

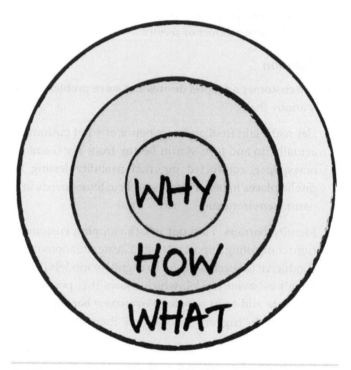

Get them to understand what you do, and why and how you do it.

"Efforts and courage are not enough without purpose and direction."
—John F. Kennedy, 35th president of the United States

The Problem

Stakeholders don't understand what teams do, so they look elsewhere to invest their time and money.

The Solution

Clearly define your team's purpose and process. Show how it fits within the overall business model.

- Be easily understood. Write a mission statement that clearly illustrates how you intend to meet business and customer needs. Make this your mantra and publicize it. Clarify key roles and responsibilities within the team so there is no misunderstanding about who does what.

- Create a set of design principles and make them measurable.[10] I always assign measurable metrics to applied principles to make them easier to understand and more tangible to an organization. For example, simplicity can be measured via a metric such as "Provide one-click purchasing from any page to reduce time to purchase by fifty percent."

- Be consistent.[11] Create a strong brand that permeates everything you and your team do. All marketing, branding, stationery, photos, illustrations, presentations, and talks should have a consistent look and feel so there is no mistaking that they are from your team. Don't send out confusing or mixed messages; they make you look unprofessional.

---

10. https://www.vitsoe.com/gb/about/good-design
11. http://www.inc.com/guides/2010/11/how-to-maintain-brand-consistency-across-product-lines.html

Ingredient 4

Know What You Control

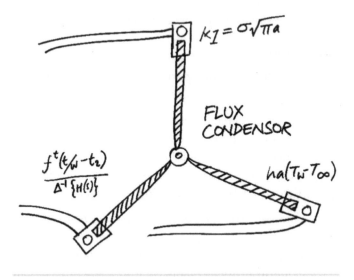

It's useless if no one can build it.

"The unexamined life is not worth living."
—Socrates, philosopher

The Problem

Organizations see delays in projects because they don't identify vital dependencies before starting.

The Solution

Identify risks, assumptions, issues, and dependencies that may cause you to fail.

- Conduct a pre-mortem.[12] Using experiences from similar projects is a good way to identify risks, assumptions, issues, and dependencies early and assess their impact hypothetically, before they happen.

- Get answers. Use exploratory testing to uncover problems.[13] Establish what you will lose if you don't fully understand unknown risks or assumptions, especially if you have a feeling they will influence the success of your project.

- Get help. Identify allies you can work with. Don't do it all yourself if someone else can do it better for you. Make a list of preferred partners and technology, then highlight the strengths and weaknesses of each to help you choose who and what is most appropriate when the time comes. Focus on what you can influence directly and let people you trust help you with everything else.

---

12. http://www.gogamestorm.com/?p=483
13. http://pragprog.com/book/ehxta/explore-it

Ingredient 5

Find the Sweet Spot

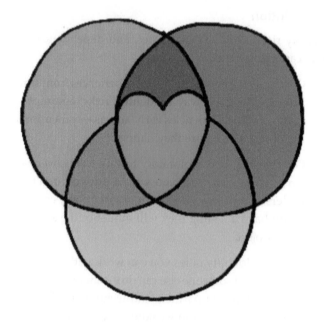

Work on things that end up in the middle.

"Ability is nothing without opportunity."
—Napoleon Bonaparte, emperor of France 1804–1815

The Problem

Companies struggle to come up with the next Facebook, Twitter, or Google but fail to realize these companies didn't try to be like anyone else.

The Solution

Look at changes in technology, human psychology, and economics to create opportunities to try something new.

- Stay informed. Up-to-date resources in the form of papers, websites, blogs, books, seminars, competitor analyses, trend reports, and trade shows are abundant. I attend events and absorb RSS feeds that align with my professional interests, always looking for new opportunities, especially ones the competition has overlooked.[14]

- Be curious and open-minded. Don't be set in your own ways; instead, put your beliefs aside and observe the world with an untainted perspective. I look for what other people are interested in and ask "why" and "what if" when I challenge my teams to notice something different.

- Look across markets. Don't limit your sources of inspiration and miss important changes in customer behavior. Look to new markets where other customers are already showing interest in a particular area. I love talking to new clients in new industries to see if I can help them to evolve their existing brands and future vision.

---

14. http://flipboard.com/

Ingredient 6

Connect the Dots

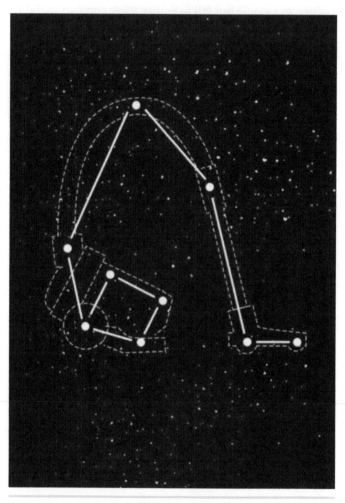

James Dyson created thousands of vacuum-cleaner prototypes before finding the perfect one.

"A discovery is said to be an accident meeting a prepared mind."
—Albert Szent-Györgyi, physiologist and Nobel Prize laureate

The Problem

Companies fail to realize the potential of putting the right technology, people, customer needs, and business goals together.

The Solution

Combine what makes sense to achieve success, and highlight the risks of not connecting the dots.

- Learn from the past. Create a knowledge-management tool to help your team find, reuse, and adapt insights from the past.[15] Different departments will also find it useful for locating design best practices and usability reports. Job done.

- Start small. Prove smaller ideas can be successful before attacking bigger assumptions and ideas. Whisk, for instance, is a mobile app that started as a simple ingredient-matching service and now has powerful semantic and linguistic analysis to improve recipe recommendations.[16]

- Affect the bigger picture. Assess the impact of changes holistically.[17] Aim to own strategic changes across all customer experiences to better advise stakeholders on which projects make sense to be worked on next.

15. http://www.forbes.com/sites/lisaquast/2012/08/20/why-knowledge-management-is-important-to-the-success-of-your-company/
16. http://thenextweb.com/apps/2013/01/09/whisk-creates-shopping-lists-based-on-recipes-and-lets-you-but-ingredients-directly-from-the-app/?fromcat=all
17. http://www.uxmatters.com/mt/archives/2011/01/barriers-to-holistic-design-solutions.php

Ingredient 7

Know What Competitors Are Up To

Anticipate what's coming.

"A wise man gets more use from his enemies than a fool from his friends."
—Baltasar Gracián, Jesuit and writer

The Problem

Companies fail to capitalize on great opportunities until it's too late.

The Solution

Conduct competitor analysis and try to stay one step ahead at all times.

- Become a customer. Experience a competitor's products and services. Try to get feedback from other customers, too, and compare product offerings using benchmarking tests to highlight deficiencies as well as areas for improvement.[18]

- Monitor social media. Track brand sentiment across popular social networks. Compare customer-service quality and response times. I always recommend social networks like Facebook as an effective way to handle customer-service issues.[19]

- Do it first. Create, combine, remove, or change functionality while factoring in market opportunities and the latest customer trends, especially ones competitors are aware of. Try to reduce your team's cycle time to deliver on competitors' own promises first and in a better way.[20]

---

18. http://www.userzoom.co.uk/ux-resources/12-questions-answered-ux-bench-marking
19. http://mashable.com/2012/04/19/facebook-customer-service-tips/
20. http://www.isixsigma.com/methodology/project-management/how-to-improve-project-cycle-time/

Start with the End

Have a clear picture of what you need to do.

"Imagination is everything. It is the preview of life's upcoming attractions."
—Albert Einstein, theoretical physicist

The Problem

If teams can't see what they're aiming for, they'll never build it right.

The Solution

Clarify the end goal and reduce risk by managing change effectively.

- Create a press release. Make an announcement to convey the benefits and value of what you are building. I regularly remind people that they are creating something important. Amazon did this with the Kindle Fire.[21]

- Clarify roles and responsibilities. List what you need to do each step of the way, and decide who is responsible for delivering each crucial part. Check to make sure team members are happy to be accountable for relevant business, development, and design decisions. A RACI (Responsible, Accountable, Consulted, and Informed) matrix is a great way to get an overview of what roles are required at key stages of a project.[22]

- Beware of moving goal posts. You can manage scope creep by getting stakeholders to sign off on clear requirements.[23] Changes and additional work are OK; just be sure to realign expectations accordingly and keep them up-to-date on your progress.

---

21. http://thenextweb.com/gadgets/2012/11/20/kindle-fire-hd-amazon-works-backwards/
22. http://www.projectsmart.co.uk/raci-matrix.html
23. http://bhusanchand.blogspot.co.uk/2010/04/scope-management-how-projects-result.html

Ingredient 9

Get Your Facts Right

Garbage in, garbage out

"An empty head is not really empty; it is stuffed with rubbish. Hence the difficulty of forcing anything into an empty head."
—Eric Hoffer, writer and Presidential Medal of Freedom award winner

The Problem

Fixing the wrong problems is expensive.

The Solution

Source the correct information before starting any project.

- Bring your research data up-to-date. Conduct user observations to see how customers perform important tasks.[24] Take note of surprising insights and remove things that no longer hold true.

- Define the problem type.[25] For example, are you increasing the speed of downloads or the accuracy of the information being returned? Challenge and reset expectations so you get the information you really need.

- Raise the quality bar.[26] Create guidelines and set up thresholds to filter out insufficient and poor-quality information. Reduce errors down the line by increasing the accuracy and depth of information needed, then having conversations in person to align expectations in order to correctly achieve desired design experiences.

---

24. http://www.usabilitynet.org/tools/userobservation.htm
25. http://www.problemsolving2.com/problem_types/dilemmas.htm
26. http://www.extremeprogramming.org/rules/functionaltests.html

Ingredient 10

Improve vs. Differentiate

Make it fit the purpose.

"Let him who would enjoy a good future waste none of his present."
—Roger Babson, educator and business theorist

The Problem

Organizations can't decide how best to remain competitive.

The Solution

Consider the past, present, and future.

- Look at the past. Review previous case studies and understand why they failed.[27] Decide if it was because of bad timing, a wrong approach, or unavailable technology. Use these insights and see if they can be applied more effectively today.

- Look at the present. Conduct market research to highlight opportunities to pivot or to improve ideas.[28] Understand what's trending outside your industry, too; leverage macro trends (for example, crowdsourcing and gamification[29]) that customers are actively involved in and see if you can incorporate them into your current scope of work.

- Look to the future. Once you've brainstormed a vision, try creating a purpose-alignment chart to visually position these new ideas.[30] This will help stakeholders understand the value and prioritize which are the most important ideas. Remove anything that doesn't differentiate or improve your current brand or product offering, and keep what you need to remain competitive.

---

27. http://www.designcouncil.org.uk/Case-studies/
28. http://www.forbes.com/sites/martinzwilling/2011/09/16/top-10-ways-entrepreneurs-pivot-a-lean-startup/
29. http://mashable.com/category/gamification/
30. http://www.beyondrequirements.com/purpose-based-alignment-model/

Ingredient 11

Do the Opposite

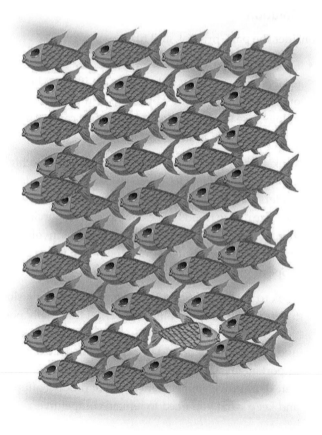

Start swimming in a different direction.

"Live your beliefs and you can turn the world around."
—Henry David Thoreau, author, poet, and philosopher

The Problem

Companies that continue doing what they've always done find it hard to innovate.

The Solution

Get your team to challenge the status quo to create something less predictable.

- Change a belief. Identify one thing that can greatly improve what you do today, even if you don't think it will work. Deliberately create a problem scenario and come up with as many solutions as possible—for example, if it's hard to decide what to eat on your own, would it be possible to use an individual's graph profile, location, and crowdsourced recommendations to suggest new places to go on a mobile device?

- Oppose an opponent. Find a competitor and do things differently. Apple's focus on creating beautiful software was born from the need to oppose Microsoft's more feature-rich approach. Even their TV commercials advised, "Think Different."[31]

- Embrace the impossible. Suspend disbelief and aim for a goal that goes against reason and feasibility. Envision how a problem can be solved using the power of design fiction.[32]

---

31. http://www.forbes.com/sites/onmarketing/2011/12/14/the-real-story-behind-apples-think-different-campaign/

32. http://www.slate.com/blogs/future_tense/2012/03/02/bruce_sterling_on_design_fictions_.html

Ingredient 12

Make It an Adventure

Inspire your team to go all the way.

"The desire to reach for the stars is ambitious. The desire to reach hearts is wise."
—Maya Angelou, author and poet

The Problem

If it's not interesting, teams won't put in everything required to see it succeed.

The Solution

Get your team members to identify with the cause so they willingly invest their time and effort.

- Improve people. Use projects to help employees achieve personal goals and beliefs. A classic Harvard study entitled "Breakthrough in On-the-Job Training" proves how training employees to become more capable while delivering a project reduces time to market, increases job satisfaction, and cuts training costs significantly.[33]

- Show the path to success. Outline each milestone, showing what team members need to do to get there. Celebrate each achievement and remind them of what still lies ahead and how much closer they are. Give them a clear road map to guide them closer to the end, one step at a time.

- Walk the talk.[34] Show them how much time or money you are willing to put in personally to make the project a success. I believe in ideas, so I am happy to put time and money into projects I am passionate about. If you do this, people will naturally want to get more involved.

---

33. http://hbr.org/1966/07/breakthrough-in-on-the-job-training/ar/1
34. http://www.uic.edu/depts/hr/mycareer/development/ZFA-9-Behaviors.pdf

Build an A-Team

Look for misfits who complement each other.

"The main ingredient of stardom is the rest of the team."
—John Wooden, basketball coach

The Problem

It's hard to find people with the right skills to deliver what you need.

The Solution

Pull together the best team you can. Work together to improve quality, trust, and industry expertise.

- Look for volunteers. Find people who want to be involved, are self-motivated, and are hungry to prove themselves. For instance, Zappos pays employees to quit, but not many do—it's a great way to test and keep only the staff members who genuinely want to stay.[35]

- Give and take feedback. Trust team members to do what's necessary, but be aware of their responsibilities, too. Challenge new teams to give constructive feedback about each other's roles until it is crystal-clear there are no skill or procedural gaps. Set the right expectations when you hire people, and make sure your entire team is aware of what has been agreed upon to avoid any confusion later on.[36]

- Train as a team. Run team-building exercises to build trust and foster a spirit of collaboration. These exercises will help the team solve problems, better understand each other, and agree how best to work more creatively and efficiently.

---

35. http://blogs.hbr.org/taylor/2008/05/why_zappos_pays_new_employees.html
36. http://www.howto.gov/web-content/governance/roles-and-responsibilities/position-descriptions

Clarify Roles and Responsibilities

Everyone has a role to play. Make sure you know yours.

"Knowing yourself is the beginning of all wisdom."
—Aristotle, philosopher

The Problem

Project teams don't know how to work well together.

The Solution

Openly discuss issues and goals before deciding what's needed to improve working relationships.

- Create a RACI (Responsible, Accountable, Consulted, and Informed) matrix to clearly show when each member of the project team is expected to be responsible, accountable, consulted, and informed at key stages in a project's life cycle.[37]

- Form roles around interests and strengths. Find out what motivates people, and let roles naturally evolve over time to keep employees happy. Challenge any ambiguity until it's crystal-clear what people are expected to do. Remove doubt and insecurity by resetting expectations as soon as possible.

- Get psychological. The Myers-Briggs personality test is an effective way of better understanding how team members and stakeholders deal with different situations based on their psychological makeup.[38] Find out what yours is and share it with your team so you can start to understand how to work better together.

37. http://www.projectsmart.co.uk/raci-matrix.html
38. http://www.myersbriggs.org/

Ingredient 15

Simplify Your Business Model

Know how your business makes money.

"Drive thy business or it will drive thee."
—Benjamin Franklin, US Founding Father

The Problem

Organizations aren't clear enough about how they make money.

The Solution

Clarify how value and costs are built up so teams know what to do to keep the business running efficiently.

- Give an overview. Use a tool like the Business Model Canvas to outline how your company plans to spend money and generate revenue.[39] List your value proposition and show how each part of the business model works to support success.

- Show customer success equals business success. Show the link between important customer and business requirements using a customer-value matrix.[40] Define the customer value you're creating and prioritize it based on return on investment.

- Highlight what's different. Many businesses can have the same model but still be differentiated. An elevator pitch is the quickest way to justify and clearly explain what customer need you are satisfying and how it meets business needs in a unique way.[41] Try writing a short sentence to highlight a key value proposition that differentiates you from competitors.

---

39. http://www.businessmodelgeneration.com/canvas
40. http://www.uxmatters.com/mt/archives/2008/12/communicating-customer-and-business-value-with-a-value-matrix.php
41. http://www.gogamestorm.com/?p=125

Pitch the Problem

Don't solve problems that don't exist.

"The single biggest problem in communication is the illusion that it has taken place."
—George Bernard Shaw, playwright, and cofounder of the London School of Economics

The Problem

Teams end up solving the wrong problems because they didn't clarify what the problem was in the first place.

The Solution

Identify a problem and agree that it exists before going any further.

- Back it up with data. Analyze usage data and market research to highlight where problems actually exist. Identify key metrics that need improving, and get the business to agree on the most important ones.

- Gain empathy. Get stakeholders and investors to identify with the problem as if it were their own.[42] Explain the risks and the rewards and show how stakeholders can personally get involved and reap the rewards. Let them hear testimonials and watch usability-testing videos to connect directly with customer needs.

- Make it obvious. Draw a direct correlation between the solution you will provide and the complete removal of the problem. Show how your business model cleverly links together customer needs, market opportunities, and trends.[43] Make your ideas tangible, as if they already exist.

---

42. http://www.agilemodeling.com/essays/activeStakeholderParticipation.htm
43. http://blogcustomermanagement-nl.bearingpoint.com/digital-innovation-needs-to-move-beyond-the-next-clever-product/

Ingredient 17

Sell It in One Sentence

Get to the point quickly.

"If I can't picture it, I can't understand it."
—Albert Einstein, theoretical physicist

The Problem

Customers don't understand what companies do, so they don't bother using their services.

The Solution

Make your value proposition obvious and easy to understand.

- Create an elevator pitch to sum up what you do.[44] Keep it really simple. Focus on an important customer need. Describe how your service meets this need in a unique way that differentiates you from a major competitor.

- Map the competition. Plot your service and your competitors' onto a value map. Choose two value attributes—for example, speed and accuracy—and show your service sits in the top right of the graph, emphasizing your unique selling point.[45]

- Have a slogan that captures your brand essence.[46] Nike has "Just Do It," which fits with the company's "don't think too much; give it a go" outlook on life and sports. What could yours be?

---

44. http://www.gogamestorm.com/?p=125
45. http://blog.kissmetrics.com/unique-selling-proposition/
46. http://www.adslogans.co.uk/hof/top10.html

Ingredient 18

Time It Right

Be at the right place at the right time, doing the right thing.

"Timing is everything. Nothing else matters."
—Anonymous

The Problem

Organizations launch ideas and improvements too late or too early.

The Solution

Conduct customer research and get enough support across your organization to prioritize work more effectively.

- Embrace relevant trends. Analyze changes in customer behavior and make a list of new trends that look like they will continue to grow. Interview, run surveys, and conduct focus groups to validate early assumptions and help narrow down your choices.

- Confirm priorities. Align your work to meet the most important business needs, and confirm they match genuine customer needs, too. Keep a close watch on the competition and what they are up to in similar areas to create a better, more well-timed proposition.

- Create early prototypes to constantly validate ideas. Improve and increase feature functionality and fidelity over time. Build momentum through this continuous learning and iterative improvement process until you have enough experience backed up by customer validation and business buy-in to launch.

Ingredient 19

Test Your Biggest Hypothesis First

Ben Franklin proved lightning is electricity.

"If we worked on the assumption that what is accepted as true really is true, then there would be little hope for advance."
—Orville Wright, inventor and aviation pioneer

The Problem

Teams don't test often or early enough, making it difficult to fix problems later.

The Solution

Create experiences to test risky assumptions. Use what you learn to create useful products.

- Do it quickly. Identify assumptions and test them immediately. This may be a high-risk new idea or technology with many dependencies. I love going to hack events like Startup Weekend because they demonstrate how quickly business concepts can be created - and pitched—in most instances, in less than forty-eight hours.[47]

- Keep it simple. Interview and conduct usability studies to get customer feedback early. Don't overengineer prototypes; create the lowest-fidelity prototype you need to successfully get an idea across. I have created early versions of ideas as a single web page, a video animation, and even a one-paragraph description.[48] Start small and build from there.

- Improve quickly. Analyze results and gain just enough insight to learn what to do next. Make changes immediately and allocate enough time to make improvements and test again. Adopt a lean-startup mentality: build, measure, and learn.[49]

---

47. http://startupweekend.org
48. http://techcrunch.com/2011/10/19/dropbox-minimal-viable-product/
49. http://theleanstartup.com/principles

Take a Leap of Faith

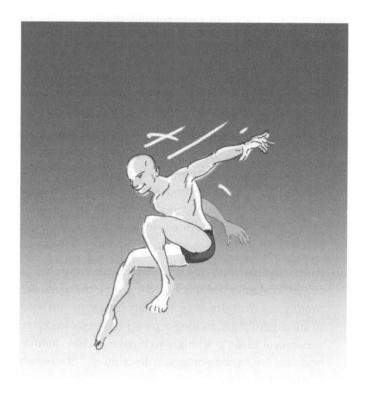

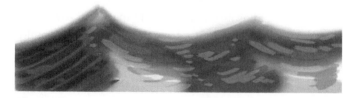

Believe in what will come.

"Faith is taking the first step even when you don't see the whole staircase."
—Martin Luther King, Jr., clergyman, activist, and leader in the African-American civil-rights movement

The Problem

No one wants to work on game-changing ideas; they are afraid to take unnecessary risks.

The Solution

Commit your team to take on a big challenge. Prepare for the journey that lies ahead.

- Stop making excuses.[50] Not ready yet? Need more training? Too risky? Make do with the team, time, and technology you can get. Treat the project as an experiment and set out to prove what works. Gain insight from both success and failure.

- Step forward. Let stakeholders know you are interested in pushing the limits of what's possible. Find like-minded people who you trust can do the job and can commit to see it through.[51]

- Get wise. Find an industry mentor and business advisor who can give you strategic advice.[52] Experience and in-depth knowledge will help you avoid pitfalls and guide you successfully to the finish line.

---

50. http://www.forbes.com/sites/kathycaprino/2012/12/28/the-8-most-damaging-excuses-people-make-for-their-unhappiness/
51. http://www.forbes.com/sites/alanhall/2012/06/04/are-you-an-entrpreneur-the-leap-of-faith/
52. http://www.kaizen-training.com/mentor-or-sponsor-%E2%80%93-are-you-getting-the-support-you-need

Part II

Ingredients to Keep You Going

Ingredient 21

Know What Will Help You Succeed

Don't wait for success. Go find it instead.

"What's missing isn't the ideas…it's the will to execute them."
—Seth Godin, entrepreneur, author, and public speaker

The Problem

Teams aren't ready when once-in-a-lifetime opportunities come their way.

The Solution

Identify what you need to have in place to help you tackle awesome opportunities that present themselves.

- Stay up-to-date. Remain abreast of the latest industry happenings, new exciting technologies, and interesting customer trends. Run competitor benchmarking to identify crucial areas you can improve to remain competitive. Strengthen your ideas and make them even more useful. Analyze what's going on so you can select the best course of action.

- Team up. Conduct a heuristic review of your current offerings. Hire in the skills to provide unbiased recommendations you can act upon if you need to. I partner with subject-matter experts to deliver innovative world-class products.[53] There is no way I can gain their knowledge overnight.

- Learn and improve quickly. Run customer research and usability tests to ensure your ideas get feedback from real customers. Validate your assumptions and remove, improve, or add to a prioritized list of features. Continue to improve and validate your ideas.[54]

---

53. http://www.forbes.com/sites/work-in-progress/2013/01/17/five-alternatives-to-a-business-partner-for-entrepreneurs-who-dont-want-to-work-solo/

54. http://www.nngroup.com/articles/iterative-design/

Put It into Context

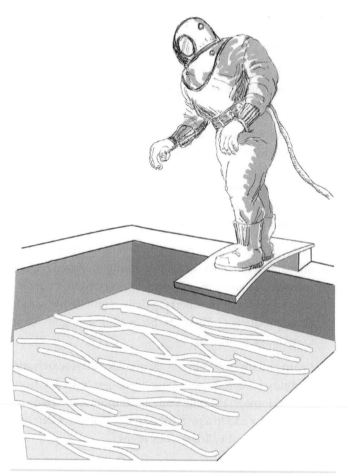

See if your solution works in the right setting.

"An inconvenience is only an adventure wrongly considered; an adventure is an inconvenience rightly considered."
—Gilbert K. Chesterton, writer

The Problem

Teams don't consider the environments in which their solutions will be used, so they create the wrong solutions.

The Solution

Know where and how your ideas will be used so you can design a better solution.

- Clarify the real goals. Find problems that need to be solved by observing what customers do. Interview them, too, and get them to prioritize what's most important.[55] Get stakeholders to do the same from a business perspective.

- Immerse yourself in the environment. Adapt your ideas to make them more suitable based on where they need to exist.[56] Let customers come to grips with your great new product by testing it where it will actually be used.

- Keep checking. Constantly validate changes to your product with customers to make sure the goals are still being met. Build and iteratively improve your product until it becomes really useful, matching customer needs as well as business needs.[57]

55. http://blogs.pmi.org/blog/voices_on_project_management/2012/10/5-steps-to-master-requirements.html
56. http://www.forbes.com/sites/shelisrael/2012/07/06/taking-google-glasses-in-context/
57. http://www.infoentrepreneurs.org/en/guides/know-your-customers--needs/

Ingredient 23

Sympathize with the Situation

Offering help at the wrong time only increases frustration.

"Let us train our minds to desire what the situation demands."
—Lucius Annaeus Seneca, philosopher

The Problem

Organizations come across as incompetent and insensitive when they provide customers with incorrect, unwanted, and untimely advice.

The Solution

Understand what customers feel under specific circumstances to deliver more-appropriate experiences.[58]

- Ask them what they want. Understand a customer's frame of mind at the start of an interaction. Try using a wizard interface to capture their feelings.[59] Show how answering questions will reduce the options and get them closer to their goal.

- Give them the right help when they need it. Start by offering clear signposting and useful advice on each key page. If customers continue to struggle, pop up a contextual help page. If it really gets bad, let them chat directly with a customer-service agent.

- Show what others feel. Incorporate peer validation. Customers find it comforting to know what someone else did to solve a problem in a situation similar to the one they are in. This form of crowdsourcing is effective when customers need peer input to make difficult decisions.[60]

---

58. http://www.psy.gla.ac.uk/~steve/hawth.html
59. http://designinginterfaces.com/patterns/wizard/
60. http://blog.mainstreethost.com/four-recent-examples-of-clever-crowdsourcing-campaigns#.UWK6RatAQwQ

Ingredient 24

They Can't Be Good at Everything

Clarify what people are supposed to be good at.

"Power of generalizing gives men so much the superiority in mistake over the dumb animals."
—George Eliot, writer

The Problem

Companies hire subject-matter experts only to find out that they aren't good in the roles they need to play.

The Solution

Avoid the "halo effect," which can bias your judgment of a person's capability based on your overall impression of the person. Verify how competent people really are in the specific environments you expect them to perform in.[61]

- Focus on strengths. Don't give employees responsibilities they're not comfortable with. For instance, Yahoo! hired Marissa Mayer as its CEO for what she was good at, not what they wanted her to be good at.[62]

- Deal with weaknesses. Use a RACI (Responsible, Accountable, Consulted, and Informed) matrix that maps out roles and responsibilities to identify missing skills or skill gaps, then find team members or external resources who can fill them.[63]

- Create advocates. User-experience (UX) designers are a minority in tech companies. An appreciation of design best practices, together with some training, empowers other team members to champion the need for good UX, complete low-level design tasks, improve productivity, and foster a sense of joint responsibility.[64]

---

61. http://en.wikipedia.org/wiki/Halo_effect
62. http://www.forbes.com/sites/greatspeculations/2012/09/07/mayer-strives-to-change-yahoo-culture/
63. http://www.projectsmart.co.uk/raci-matrix.html
64. http://uxdesign.smashingmagazine.com/2012/08/29/beyond-wireframing-real-life-ux-design-process/

Be a Catalyst

Show people what they're missing.

"I am certainly not one of those who need to be prodded. In fact, if anything, I am the prod."
—Winston Churchill, prime minister of the United Kingdom, 1940–1945 and 1951–1955

The Problem

Great ideas get diluted when there isn't anyone to keep things moving along.

The Solution

Place strong leaders and skilled people in your organization to influence and guide teams to be more successful.

- Give context. Provide enough relevant background information—including trend analysis, industry insight, and customer behaviors—to inform design, technical, and business decisions. You can use personas to help teams justify what they are building, matching features to real user needs and expectations.[65]

- Show them. Introduce your team to techniques that can better generate, prioritize, and shape ideas. Mentor teams to complete tasks using the new techniques they have learned to come up with relevant solutions.[66] The best way to learn is through practice.

- Stoke the fire. Nudge team members along to come up with interesting and creative solutions. Challenge original stakeholders' needs and surprise them with newer, more-relevant ideas. Refer back to goals to check if they have really been met. If not, get back on track quickly. I love holding ice-breaker meetings at strategic points of a project to get the creative juices flowing again.[67]

---

65. http://uxmag.com/articles/personas-the-foundation-of-a-great-user-experience
66. http://adaptivemarketing.in/usability-and-interface-design-workshop
67. http://www.mindtools.com/pages/article/newLDR_76.htm

Perform as a Team

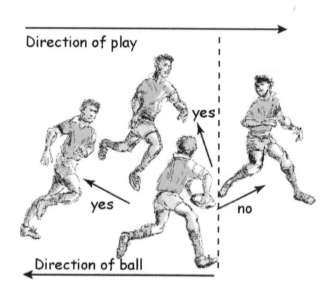

Direction of play

yes

yes

no

Direction of ball

Trust team members to play their parts.

"You may have the greatest bunch of individual stars in the world, but if they don't play together, the club won't be worth a dime."
—Babe Ruth, baseball player

The Problem

Companies with the best teams in the world still fail to deliver anything great.

The Solution

Learn to work better as a team by appreciating and supporting each other to achieve success in the best possible ways. A team that plays well together performs well together.

- Be confident. The Pygmalion or Rosenthal effect proves that the greater the expectation placed on a group of individuals, the better they perform.[68] It's helpful to discuss what each team member wants to do, then support and convince him or her that it's possible.

- Have goals. Be clear about what needs to be achieved and keep your team informed. Hold regular review sessions to go through new requirements and changes based on feedback from usability testing. I find cross-discipline pairing the best way to reduce confusion, improve productivity, and lessen the need for unnecessary documentation.[69]

- Be efficient. Leverage individual strengths and weaknesses by all means, but don't forget softer skills, too. I covet essential traits like collaboration, communication, creativity, and flexibility,[70] without which a team can not perform efficiently.

---

68. http://ideas.time.com/2013/04/01/how-to-use-the-pygmalion-effect/
69. http://online.wsj.com/article/
     SB10000872396390443855804577599993053055030.html
70. http://www.forbes.com/sites/kevinkruse/2012/12/26/ibm-ceo-study/

Fight Them to Know Them

It's OK to get hurt as long as you learn from it.

"As our enemies have found, we can reason like men, so now let us show them we can fight like men also."
—Thomas Jefferson, US Founding Father

The Problem

Teams don't challenge each other and stakeholders, so they end up delivering solutions that just don't hit the mark.

The Solution

Get emotional and get frustrated. Show you care, and push people on your team and within your organization to be the best they can be.

- Ask for a slap in the face. Question what's wrong, not what's right. Highlight mistakes and focus on the learning gained through failure to explore new directions. Let your enemies teach you a lesson or two, and keep them close—just make sure you get up and keep going.[71]

- Put your foot down. Give team members and stakeholders constructive feedback and monitor the impact on performance—for example, a reduction in errors.[72] Agile development practices encourage conversations over documentation; having regular retrospectives and daily stand-ups gives everyone the opportunity to openly discuss how the project and team are performing.

- Hire annoying people.[73] If you hire like-minded people, everyone will agree on the same suggestions. Work with people who like to challenge the status quo and who are willing to fight for what they believe in. It doesn't matter if they rub you the wrong way as long as it encourages healthy debate and diverse ideas.

---

71. http://thefuturebuzz.com/2010/04/12/why-you-need-enemies/
72. http://www.dummies.com/how-to/content/giving-constructive-feedback.html
73. http://www.fastcompany.com/3000966/why-hiring-people-who-annoy-you-helps-you-innovate

Just Flow with It

Make it as easy as rowing a boat downstream.

"Success usually comes to those who are too busy to be looking for it."
—Henry David Thoreau, author, poet, and philosopher

The Problem

People struggle when they do things they don't enjoy.

The Solution

Get your team to buy in to their work and inspire them to be the best they can be by playing to their strengths and interests so they are superfocused and extremely satisfied with all that they do.[74]

- Become valuable.[75] We can't always be in the perfect job. But we can make it easier and more enjoyable. Try to understand the background of every project you work on, locating interesting information to stay motivated. Show initiative and become the person people go to for knowledge and clarification.

- Do what you love.[76] If you've tried to make the situation better and had little success, look elsewhere. Find more-interesting projects, work with a new team, and invest your time and energy in a cause you truly believe in. Do what you can to get more motivated, satisfied, and financially better off.

- Align with a higher purpose.[77] Requirements and goals may change, but keep your team focused on the overarching vision. Empower teams to make changes based on this vision, and get them to challenge themselves and others to do what's best to stay aligned with the vision.

---

74. http://en.wikipedia.org/wiki/Mihaly_Csikszentmihalyi
75. http://www.forbes.com/sites/jacquelynsmith/2012/12/18/14-ways-to-be-better-at-your-job-in-2013/
76. http://www.businessnewsdaily.com/3191-reasons-to-do-what-you-love.html
77. http://www.infoq.com/articles/agile-goal-setting-appelo

Ingredient 29

Train Them Right

Give people the skills and motivation to succeed.

"By failing to prepare, you are preparing to fail."
—Benjamin Franklin, US Founding Father

The Problem

Team members fail to complete tasks because they don't know how to do them.

The Solution

Get teams the required training to perform well.

- Motivate them.[78] Understand what drives people, and create incentives to attract their interest. You can ask team members what they hope to get out of a project and give them a choice of rewards that reflect their needs. This shared agreement enables stakeholders and teams to focus on delivering the right things for the right reasons.

- Show them how. Empower employees to apply learning to real-life situations. I mentor startups and technology teams, giving them the theory behind a technique, then work with them to apply the techniques practically and successfully. Give them the skills and confidence to apply techniques on their own, but know how to guide without restricting them.[79]

- Reveal the path. Give people a road map they can apply, evolve, and adapt. Encourage team members to use the knowledge they have, but also show them what success is—what the next steps are and how many steps remain —so they aren't left wondering. Make it easy for them to progress.

---

78. http://www.behaviormodel.org/
79. http://ecaminc.com/index.php/blog/59-generalblog/191-2010-03-22

Ingredient 30

Make It Easy

If there is an easier way, do it that way.

"The less effort, the faster and more powerful you will be."
—Bruce Lee, martial artist

The Problem

Teams try to do too much at the same time, so they end up delivering below-par results, leaving customers and investors confused and disappointed.

The Solution

Help your team complete tasks as easily as possible by finding the path of least resistance.

- Simplify decisions. Don't make things harder than they need to be. Refer to Occam's razor as a heuristic to find the fewest assumptions and risks needed to proceed with your project.[80] If off-the-shelf software is just as good, cheaper, and easier to integrate, use it instead of building your own.

- Do less. Expending extra effort increases the likelihood that you'll be unable to complete a project. Promise less to start with, and overdeliver. Add functionality once you know it is needed. Do less to achieve more by managing complexity.[81] Get rid of unnecessary functionality or processes.

- Give examples. Use relevant case studies to show your team and other stakeholders how new ideas have been successfully applied before. Refer to best practices they can access, adopt, and use to justify decisions. Make it as easy as possible for teams to understand, apply, and discover what's possible until they are capable and motivated enough to continually apply the ideas themselves.

---

80. http://www.webdesignerdepot.com/2010/07/occams-razor-a-great-principle-for-designers/
81. http://blogs.hbr.org/ashkenas/2011/02/the-c-level-job-for-everyone-r.html

Ingredient 31

Prioritize Ideas

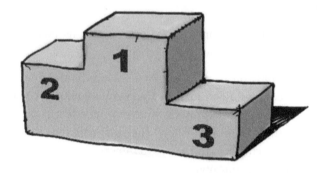

Know what will get you first place.

"The most urgent decisions are rarely the most important ones."
—Dwight D. Eisenhower, five-star general and 34th president of the United States

The Problem

Companies make bad choices because they don't know what's really important.

The Solution

Assign business success metrics and customer values to ideas to see if they're worth pursuing.

- Take a guess. Get your team to estimate the relative effort to deliver each idea, and get stakeholders to verify business success metrics. Use simple games like Planning Poker.[82]

- Let ideas compete. Use a value graph to get an overview of which ideas are best.[83] Put important business criteria like "Return on Investment" (ROI) and "Effort" on the x- and y-axes. Map ideas onto the graph and see which ones offer the best ROI with the least effort. Don't forget to factor in dependencies and look out for high-effort, high-ROI ideas that can lead to innovation. Decide which ones make the most sense to work on first.

- Validate early. Get customer feedback by running focus groups and usability-testing prototypes. Gain insight and reassess what is of value before deciding your next move. I encourage small, medium, and large enterprises alike to adopt the lean-startup methodology of "build, measure, learn" to help validate ideas.[84]

---

82. http://www.crisp.se/bocker-och-produkter/planning-poker
83. http://stackoverflow.com/questions/1487102/what-factors-do-you-consider-when-deciding-what-to-work-on-next
84. http://theleanstartup.com/

Ingredient 32

Slice It Thinly

Don't waste time on something that won't fit.

"If the facts don't fit the theory, change the facts."
—Albert Einstein, theoretical physicist

The Problem

Companies waste time creating really complex features no one wants. Changes later in delivery require extra time since dependencies need to be considered.

The Solution

Avoid doing too much too soon; create a simple version you can validate with real customers, early.

- Start small. Create a minimum viable product to see if a concept works or an assumption is correct.[85] This can be as simple as a link that pops up in a form to capture feedback or a video to inform customers about what your company is doing. Be careful not to confuse customers or stakeholders who might think that is all they are going to get, though.

- Do what's necessary. My rule of thumb is to create features that would render an idea useless if they were removed. Progressively disclose functionality once core pieces have proven to be useful.[86]

- Test it quickly. Guerrilla-usability-test your minimum viable product on real customers.[87] I'm quite happy to test an idea with customers in a café and reward them with cups of coffee. Give teams and stakeholders an early indication of what works to help them decide what to do next. Test breadth of functionality across the holistic experience to spot the big problems, not just the detailed ones.

---

85. http://techcrunch.com/2012/07/13/how-to-create-a-minimum-viable-product/
86. http://sixrevisions.com/user-interface/progressive-disclosure-in-user-interfaces/
87. http://www.designmap.com/practice/more-on-guerrilla-usability-really/

Ingredient 33

Find the Shortest Route

London taxis get you to your destination quickly.

"Don't keep a man guessing too long—he's sure to find the answer somewhere else."
—Mae West, actress

The Problem

In their eagerness to meet business goals, companies introduce unnecessary restrictions and rules, making it hard to get things done quickly.

The Solution

Make it easy to perform specific tasks, and give team members enough freedom to do what is best.

- Show less. Reduce the number of options and make it easy to compare the benefits, dependencies, and costs of and differences between each so that a quicker, more informed decision can be made. The $100 test, for instance, is a simple way to justify and differentiate between a small set of options.[88]

- Use shortcuts. Use a story map to prioritize important features.[89] This "must-have" set of features represents the minimum viable product your team needs to build to ensure main objectives are achieved holistically.

- Always have an answer. Solve customer and business problems as best you can. If you can't find an exact match, highlight any shortfalls or differences, as well as improvements your final solution provides. Upfront, set expectations that you plan to do this, and don't turn away users unnecessarily.

---

88. http://www.gogamestorm.com/?p=457
89. http://www.agileproductdesign.com/presentations/user_story_mapping/index.html

Timebox It

Challenge people to make decisions in meetings.

"The ultimate inspiration is the deadline."
—Nolan Bushnell, engineer, entrepreneur, and founder of Atari

The Problem

Teams spend meeting after meeting discussing ideas without making any decisions.

The Solution

Frame a lack of time as a challenge, and coach teams to do just enough to proceed to the next stage. Get the adrenaline and creative juices flowing.

- Set meaningful objectives.[90] Be clear what needs to be achieved in the time you have. You can ask individual team members to describe out loud what they think they are supposed to be doing so there is no confusion.

- Have shorter meetings.[91] Achieve as much as possible within the time allotted. Always try to wrap up a meeting in less time than scheduled. Gather enough information to make a decision, and agree on clear acceptance criteria on all agenda items so people know when they can consider a job done.

- Validate quickly. If you have time to ask only one person, ask one person! If you need to make a decision, find the easiest and most rewarding option to keep moving forward. Web-usability expert Jakob Nielsen believes you need to test with only five people.[92,93]

90. http://www.forbes.com/sites/victorlipman/2013/01/04/the-best-way-for-a-manager-to-start-the-year-set-clear-meaningful-employee-objectives/
91. http://h41112.www4.hp.com/promo/obc/za/en/business-it-advice/improve-teamwork/tips-for-smarter-meetings.html
92. http://www.nngroup.com/people/jakob-nielsen/
93. http://www.nngroup.com/articles/why-you-only-need-to-test-with-5-users/

Ingredient 35

Keep It Simple

Don't overengineer a solution if a simpler one will do.

"Life is really simple, but we insist on making it complicated."
—Confucius, teacher, politician, and philosopher

The Problem

Products and services get complicated when businesses keep adding features to please too many people at the same time.

The Solution

Deliver maximum delight by doing the least possible while meeting the most-important customer needs.

- Find out what really matters. Interview customers in their workplaces and observe how they achieve tasks naturally. Try conducting a contextual inquiry.[94] Keep testing and making improvements to your ideas until you have honed something that matches real user needs.

- Be more predictable. Reduce the time it takes to complete tasks. Make features really intuitive so there's little doubt what they are meant to do.[95] Compare qualitative as well as quantitative metrics to ensure both aspects are improved.[96]

- Get rid of it. Improve your solution's usability by keeping it light and focused. Remove anything that doesn't need to be there. Do less and focus on making your solution more usable and useful.[97] Apple's iPhone freed up hardware real estate by removing the fixed keyboard usually found on other phones, for example.[98]

---

94. http://www.usabilitynet.org/tools/contextualinquiry.htm
95. http://en.wikipedia.org/wiki/Affordance
96. http://www.nngroup.com/articles/usability-metrics/
97. http://www.uxgroundswell.com/2010/04/flexibility-usability-tradeoff/
98. http://www.apple.com/uk/pr/library/2007/01/09Apple-Reinvents-the-Phone-with-iPhone.html

Use the 80/20 Rule

Improve useful features people actually want.

"The art of being wise is knowing what to overlook."
—William James, philosopher and first educator to offer a
psychology course in the United States

The Problem

Teams waste time building complex functionality people
hardly use.

The Solution

The 80/20 rule focuses on creating and improving the twenty
percent of features that customers use eighty percent of time,
and making those experiences more useful and brilliant.[99]

- Get the basics right. Allow customers to achieve
  important repeatable tasks easily. Validate and match
  functionality and quality expectations. Add enhancements and functionality if necessary.

- Remember to make experts happy, too. Don't reveal
  additional functionality unless customers need it.
  Designers and developers can apply design heuristics
  so access to advanced features is obvious and unclut-
  tered. Don't give people too many options at any one
  time. Expert products need to be complex, though, so
  your target users can control more of their desired
  outcome.

- Evolve the most useful twenty percent. Observe what
  customers do to see if they are using your products and
  services in an unintended and productive way. Use this
  insight to enhance existing functionality and create new
  functionality, then make these changes more readily
  available.

---

99. http://www.crn.com/news/security/18821726/microsofts-ceo-80-20-rule-
applies-to-bugs-not-just-features.htm

Constrain Yourself

Restrict yourself to come up with unexpected solutions.

"Perfection is achieved not when there is nothing more to add, but when there is nothing left to take away."
—Antoine de Saint-Exupéry, aristocrat, writer, poet, and pioneering aviator

The Problem

Too much freedom of choice makes it more time-consuming and difficult for teams to decide what to build and how.

The Solution

Limit your team's access to resources and time. Do more with less to start with so you have time and money left over if you really need it later.

- Move it elsewhere. This concept is known as transposition. It involves moving established ideas and beliefs to a new domain. Yandex, for instance, used Google's business strategy and is now the biggest search engine in Russia.[100]

- Specialize and evolve. Focus on making one part of your idea the focus and the unique selling point. Invest your team's efforts in making that one part the best in the industry. Create new products and services that are higher-quality and more focused.

- Remove functionality.[101] Spot opportunities where others only see oversimplification. Replace what you remove with a really sticky factor like fun or kudos. Instagram is a good example.[102] When you distill it, it is just another photo app that allows you to add filters to pictures—but everybody uses it.

---

100. http://en.wikipedia.org/wiki/Yandex
101. http://arcball.com/2010/04/20-ways-to-find-the-simplest-design-how-to-cut-features-and-enjoy-it/
102. http://instagram.com/

Ingredient 38

Be Really Good at One Thing

Find it!

The choice is easy when you're good at one thing.

"There are three responses to a piece of design—yes, no, and WOW! Wow is the one to aim for."
—Milton Glaser, graphic designer

The Problem

Customers use competitors because it isn't clear what your organization does.

The Solution

Focus on being great at one thing to start with.

- Quality first. Analyze competitor's strengths and weaknesses and find one thing you can be much better at. An emphasis on quality allowed the Apple iPhone to revolutionize the smartphone industry with a first-class design and user experience that blew away the competition.[103]

- Be different. Be quirky, be mysterious, be surprising. Let customers remember your brand. I love Innocent Drinks and their unique take on healthy living mixed with an infectiously fun brand.[104]

- Combine strengths. Link products and services to show how they complement each other. For example, I have been using Adobe products since 1990. Adobe has the best products, each powerful in its own right but even more useful as part of a cohesive product suite.[105]

103. http://www.fastcodesign.com/1665375/the-6-pillars-of-steve-jobss-design-philosophy
104. http://www.designcouncil.org.uk/case-studies/innocent-drinks/
105. http://www.adobe.com/uk/products/creativesuite/designstandard/reviews.html

Be Unfashionable

Do the unexpected—they'll love you more for it.

"All progress has resulted from people who took unpopular positions."
—Adlai E. Stevenson II, US representative to the United Nations

The Problem

Companies try too hard to be popular and end up diluting their services to fit in.

The Solution

Please loyal customers by going over the top. Forget about anyone else; your customers need to matter the most.[106] Those who aren't customers will follow suit because they can see the care and attention you are giving those who are customers.

- Spoil them. Listen to what your most active and loyal customers want, and keep them happy by delivering experiences to meet their needs. Reward your advocates so they continue spreading the good word.[107]

- Show off. Make it obvious that you appreciate your customers. Shower your advocates and superusers with rewards and recognition. Let less-involved or newer customers see how well you look after those who are influential and loyal so they want to be those things too.

- Be extreme. Differentiate yourself from competitors as much as possible. Do things they would never dream of doing because they have too much to risk. Get known for looking after the interests of your niche audience and creating wild and wonderful experiences that only your audience would care for.[108]

---

106. http://www.forbes.com/sites/meghancasserly/2012/03/11/erika-napoletano-the-power-of-unpopular-at-sxsw/

107. http://www.forbes.com/sites/kellyclay/2012/12/15/will-2013-be-the-year-of-loyalty-programs/

108. http://www.forbes.com/sites/knowledgewharton/2011/10/06/12011/

Ingredient 40

Fail Fast, Fail Often

Try new things until you succeed.

"I didn't fail the test, I just found 100 ways to do it wrong."
—Benjamin Franklin, US Founding Father

The Problem

Many companies are still too risk-averse. They waste time overanalyzing and making incremental changes that don't really make a difference.

The Solution

Treat your projects as a series of experiments, and learn from each one. Discover valuable insights and overcome your fears by remembering that disproving a hypothesis is not a failure.

- Learn from failure.[109] When something does not work as you expected, take it as an indication of what not to do. Assess the implications and make relevant changes to focus on what customers want instead.

- Provide more-frequent updates. Run more experiments so stakeholders don't invest too much in each result.[110] Get them accustomed to using insights to make decisions more frequently.

- Recognize failure. Define tasks and metrics against which you can measure success. A failed experiment is one that doesn't produce statistically significant results for or against your hypothesis. Social-media return-on-investment success can be easily measured based on a brand's share of audience voice, conversation effectiveness, advocacy percentage, and likability compared to competitors'.[111]

---

109. http://www.forbes.com/sites/dorieclark/2013/01/03/why-failure-is-good-for-leaders/
110. http://www.forbes.com/sites/rawnshah/2012/11/02/for-innovation-knowledge-is-a-poor-substitute-for-experimentation/
111. http://mashable.com/2012/10/31/4-metrics-to-measure-social-medias-roi/

Ingredient 41

Find the Gaps

Fill in the gap before it gets bigger.

"He who knows all the answers has not been asked all the questions."
—Confucius, teacher, politician, and philosopher

The Problem

Teams leave too many questions unanswered. If you don't know what you don't know, trouble may arrive when you least expect it.

The Solution

Quickly identify what you don't know and get the answers you need before you decide what to do next.

- Catch problems early. Keep a log of new and recurring technological, environmental, social, and behavioral factors. Identify the ones that represent the biggest risks, and aim to understand their effects and deal with them before they become genuine concerns.

- Be S.M.A.R.T.[112] Once you have highlighted areas you need to address, set goals that are specific, measurable, achievable, realistic, and timely so you know you have been successful at solving them based on real metrics.

- Track holistically. Monitor changes in one area to make sure there are no adverse affects on any other part of the business or the project you are working on. In the paid-advertising world you can set up automated alerts to notify teams when there is a fluctuation in performance.[113] This allows teams to react quickly to prevent any further damage.

---

112. http://topachievement.com/smart.html
113. http://searchenginewatch.com/article/2168433/Automated-Alerts-Robotic-Guardian-Angels-of-PPC

Play a Good Game

Know the rules to navigate your way to success.

"You cannot escape the responsibility of tomorrow by evading it today."
—Abraham Lincoln, 16th president of the United States

The Problem

It takes only one mistake to rub people the wrong way so they never trust you again.

The Solution

Show respect toward key people in your organization to help you be more successful.

- Become a subject-matter expert.[114] Be prepared to back up your opinions with proof. Research the topic at hand and take note of important points you can leverage to put forward your case more convincingly.

- Find a mentor.[115] Find someone who can help you navigate through the political minefield—someone who has been through the battles. As a mentor, I guide and prepare people for situations they will come across. I offer a second opinion and push them hard.

- Learn from experience. You will not win every argument or debate. The most important thing is to gain experience and be better prepared to fight another day. Always push for a good conclusion (this may not always be yours) as long as all parties have had input and a shared consensus has been reached.

---

114. http://www.isixsigma.com/dictionary/subject-matter-expert-sme/
115. http://www.forbes.com/sites/lisaquast/2013/01/02/4-tips-for-finding-great-career-mentors/

Ingredient 43

Look for Commonalities

Learn from the past to create something new.

"The invariable mark of wisdom is to see the miraculous in the common."
—Ralph Waldo Emerson, essayist and poet

The Problem

Teams duplicate efforts because they're not aware they're working on something that has been done before.

The Solution

Research what other teams and competitors have already proved useful, and use that knowledge to inform decisions.

- Learn from past success. Find out why something worked previously. Look for opportunities to abstract or transform ideas from the past to help teams find solutions to enhance and complete requirements more quickly. Be careful not to copy an idea; always look to evolve or improve one.

- Avoid repeating mistakes.[116] Try new approaches to tackle problems while factoring in current customer trends and new technology. Past failures can be due to factors outside a team's control, so stay abreast of market conditions before deciding what to do.

- Take the best bits. Combine the best ideas and features to create a better product.[117] Improve the effectiveness of your experiences by uniting elements that complement each other. Be careful not to create a monster, though—combining too many features will decrease usability.

---

116. http://www.linkedin.com/today/post/article/20121211162106-32702694-big-idea-2013-learning-fast-from-failure
117. http://www.creativethinkingwith.com/Combine-Ideas.html

Ingredient 44

Don't Improve Only the Obvious

Don't just improve the way it looks if the rest doesn't work.

"We live in an age when unnecessary things are our only necessities."
—Oscar Wilde, writer and poet

The Problem

Teams implement common solutions without context and don't solve the real problems.

The Solution

Find and improve the things that really matter.

- Get some help. Identify important problems you have delayed attending to because your teams can't deal with them themselves. Find partners who can help you solve these problems in a timely, professional, and cost-effective way.

- Improve perceived value. Delight customers before and after a task you want them to complete. For example, give discounts or include free shipping for online purchases. Make customers aware of how much they can save so they feel good about completing their purchases.

- Step out of your comfort zone. Find inspiration in areas you don't normally look at. Improve one aspect of your product or service, using new insight, and test how big the impact is. Base changes on what customers would find most valuable, even if it means going against what you believe.

Align with Expectations

Make it easy to see what's going to happen next.

"That is a good book which is opened with expectation, and closed with delight and profit."
—Amos Bronson Alcott, teacher, writer, philosopher, and reformer

The Problem

Project costs rise when there isn't a clear project vision, scope, or delivery process.

The Solution

Agree on scope, delivery processes, and roles. Work closely and inform each other of any changes so that there are no unpleasant surprises.

- Understand everyone's role. Create a RACI (Responsible, Accountable, Consulted, and Informed) matrix to show who's needed at key project stages.[118] Keep this up-to-date and share changes with the entire team.

- Confirm the scope.[119] Agree to keep track of an up-to-date backlog. Make everyone aware of the consequence of any decision before proceeding. Work closely as a team to ensure conversations and decisions are captured and made visible to all.

- Incorporate feedback that makes a difference.[120] Show how important recommendations from usability studies, expert heuristics, and best practices have been applied to improve the project to impact key business success metrics.

---

118. http://en.wikipedia.org/wiki/Responsibility_assignment_matrix
119. http://www.uie.com/articles/collaborative_shared_understanding/
120. http://www.upassoc.org/upa_publications/jus/2007august/useful-usable.html

Ingredient 46

Attract What You Want

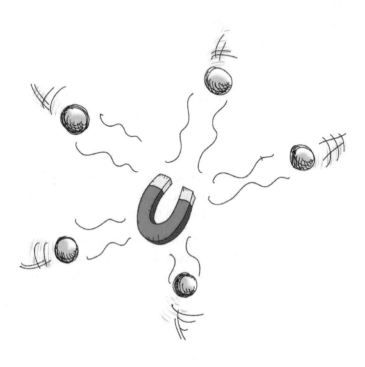

Attract the right things.

"If you don't know what you want you will always attract the wrong things in life."
—Anonymous

The Problem

Teams miss opportunities in their eagerness to reach the finish line.

The Solution

Let people know what you want, and make the benefits obvious.

- Clarify what you need.[121] Be clear about the opportunities, roles, technology, and rewards for participation. Show how a mutually beneficial relationship can be had, and ask those interested to confirm their understanding so expectations can be matched. Don't assume you know what everyone wants or that they know what they have to do.

- Plan ahead. Don't wait until it's too late to secure the money, equipment, and resources you need.[122] Make the most of the opportunity when it arrives so you can ask for more the next time.

- Put yourself out there. Approach innovative, ready-to-be-engaged companies and people,[123] and present the opportunity to get them involved. Go and get them in case they don't know who you are or what you need. Ensure a shared understanding of the goals that need to be achieved. Ask people to state them back to you in person.

---

121. http://www.inc.com/diane-zuckerman/springboard-why-you-cant-innovate-alone.html
122. http://www.businessweek.com/innovate/content/mar2011/id20110311_532002.htm
123. http://www.forbes.com/sites/tomiogeron/2013/01/15/live-facebook-announces-graph-search/

Don't Ask What They Want

Take what people want with a grain of salt.

"If I asked people what they wanted, they would have asked for a faster horse and carriage."
—Henry Ford, founder of the Ford Motor Company

The Problem

Companies rely too much on what customers think they want and not enough on what they will actually need. Customers aren't experts, so they will come up with limited and, sometimes, unrealistic suggestions.

The Solution

Observe what customers do, and come up with new ways to delight them.

- Observe customers. If you can't do it in person, video-record what they do and review it later. Get them to think out loud and explain their thoughts each step of the way.[124]

- Benchmark results.[125] Test prototypes of your ideas to capture relevant feedback. Create something tangible customers can interact with and give them tasks to complete, then assess their success based on time, accuracy, and percentage of completion.

- Don't lead. Tell them you don't expect right or wrong answers to avoid the subject-expectancy effect.[126] People choose an expected result to remain in favor with the tester. Encourage them to explore and make mistakes naturally so you can identify what really works and what doesn't.

---

124. http://www.uxmatters.com/mt/archives/2012/03/talking-out-loud-is-not-the-same-as-thinking-aloud.php
125. http://www.measuringusability.com/blog/essential-metrics.php
126. http://en.wikipedia.org/wiki/Subject-expectancy_effect

Lead by Example

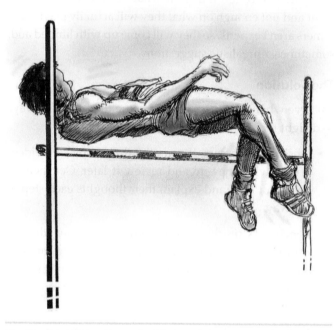

The Fosbury Flop showed athletes a better way to high-jump.

"Do not go where the path may lead; go instead where there is no path and leave a trail."
—Ralph Waldo Emerson, essayist and poet

The Problem

Teams find it difficult to apply the latest practices and techniques that have been taught to them.

The Solution

Demonstrate a hands-on approach to show people what's possible through practice.

- Teach the theory. Attend and speak at events in your area of expertise.[127] Network with industry peers and get recognized for your points of view. People will want to follow and know more about what you believe.

- Practice the theory. Run workshops and coach teams to demonstrate how techniques and skills can be applied to meet specific participant needs.[128] Make your sessions practical, fun, and memorable. Include participants in discussions and don't make it a one-way lecture purely on theory.

- Apply the theory. To prove a theory works, I find it useful to have adopted and applied it myself. This lets me feel more confident giving advice, where I can accurately show personal examples of success and failure, allowing others to learn from my firsthand experience. An example of this is a startup I created to validate the need for an artificial intelligence system to link what people talk about on social networks to interesting content they can watch, read, and buy.[129]

---

127. http://www.eewei.com/my-talks/
128. http://www.uxutsav.com/topicUxTools.html
129. http://emoti.vu

Ingredient 49

Be Prepared

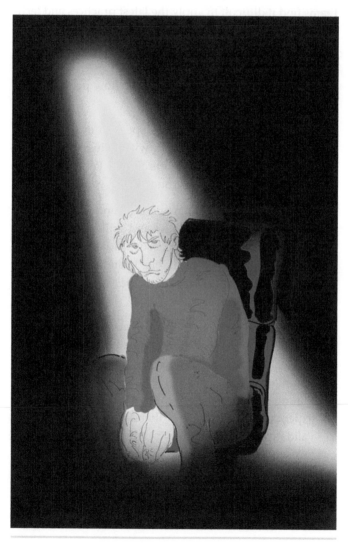

Have the answers ready.

"Whoever does not know how to hit the nail on the head should be asked not to hit it at all."
—Friedrich Nietzsche, philosopher, poet, composer, cultural critic, and classical philologist

The Problem

Teams walk into meetings without relevant and timely information to back up their decisions.

The Solution

Understand what stakeholders and customers expect, and have the answers ready.

- Know what you don't know. Build prototypes to test assumptions and surface previously unknown risks. Get answers to the questions, fill in knowledge gaps, and remove any unnecessary distractions. Stay focused and leave no stone unturned.

- Keep up-to-date. Do your homework to constantly assess the relevancy of the latest customer trends and know what competitors are up to so you can find opportunities to improve your service as much as possible.

- Deliver what's expected first. Get the basics right and match original expectations, where it makes sense, before anything else. New insights that can make a big impact should be included too, but make sure you justify their existence and show how you've prioritized these accordingly.

Frame It

Get them to see your point of view.

"Each man should frame life so that at some future hour, fact and his dreaming meet."
—Victor Hugo, poet, novelist, and dramatist of the Romantic movement

The Problem

Stakeholders don't understand what's required because they can't relate to it.

The Solution

Simplify and personalize the concept so it's easy for them to buy into the idea.

- Help them see. Tell an interesting story to vividly illustrate the points you want to get across.[130] Base it on a real-life experience if possible and keep it simple, with no more than three core benefits.

- Make it personal.[131] Show them how your solution will solve their specific problems. Let them ask questions early, and answer them with examples showing which parts of your ideas are most relevant. Get them to identify what is useful.

- Keep it simple.[132] Keep presentations and demonstrations short. Show that you understand the main requirements, and summarize key points concisely and accurately. Be genuine, not someone else, and link to relevant cultural and business references to show that what you are talking about has context.

---

130. http://www.ted.com/talks/andrew_stanton_the_clues_to_a_great_story.html
131. http://www.forbes.com/sites/trustedadvisor/2012/09/11/the-practice-of-empathy/
132. http://www.entrepreneur.com/blog/223513

Focus on the Details

Fix the little things that make a big difference.

"Great things are done by a series of small things brought together."
—Vincent van Gogh, painter

The Problem

Teams don't spend enough time making small improvements that can deliver a lot of value.

The Solution

Group and prioritize small changes, especially if they can provide as much impact as big ones but with less investment.

- Little change, big difference. Use data analytics to pinpoint where customers consistently fail in completing business-critical tasks. Identify any small improvements that can be made to get them into the next round of change requests. I use the Kano model to uncover, classify, and integrate important customer needs, creating delightful experiences that become essential through time.[133]

- Show customers you listen. Fix issues they complain about the most. Acknowledge their input with an accurate resolution and let customers rely on your team to deliver results on time every time. The Firefox Input Team does just this.[134]

- The benefits all add up. A bunch of small improvements in succession may be more effective than a single large change. Assign relative effort sizes and fix issues that require the least amount of effort for the biggest return first.[135]

---

133. http://www.kanomodel.com/
134. http://www.agilebok.org/index.php?title=Relative_Sizing_and_Story_Points
135. http://blog.mozilla.org/addons/2011/09/06/user-feedback-for-desktop-firefox-add-on-developers/

Ingredient 52

Reduce the Options

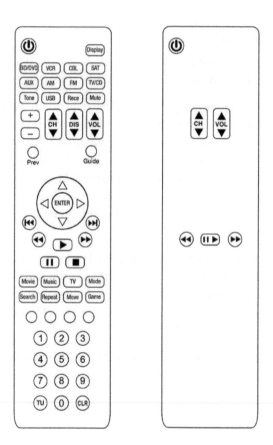

Sometimes the basics are all you need.

"Less is more."
—Ludwig Mies van der Rohe, architect

The Problem

Solutions are too complicated when customers have too many choices, making it harder for them to decide.

The Solution

Give customers more control when they need it.[136] Keep choices to a minimum to help customers make quicker decisions.

- Conduct multivariate tests.[137] Design and test different designs where the number of possible choices varies. Compare the effectiveness of each design. Implement the solution that causes the least confusion and allows customers to achieve tasks in the shortest time possible.

- Start with the basics. Understand the customer's hierarchy of needs, and design to progressively disclose additional functionality.[138] Keep unnecessary features hidden until they are required.

- Differentiate options. When designing interactions, factor in Fitt's law, which states the time required to rapidly move to a target area is a function of the distance to the target and the size of the target.[139] Locate the most useful options close together and increase the size of important functions to indicate their relevance.

136. http://en.wikipedia.org/wiki/Hick's_law
137. https://www.optimizely.com/resources/multivariate-test-vs-ab-test
138. http://codecraft.co/2012/09/16/progressive-disclosure-everywhere/
139. http://en.wikipedia.org/wiki/Fitts_law

Ingredient 53

Make It Obvious

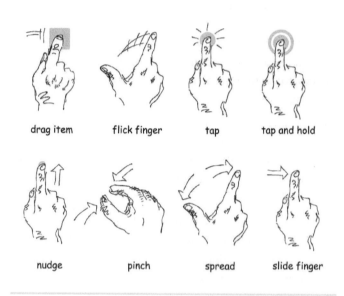

drag item   flick finger   tap   tap and hold

nudge   pinch   spread   slide finger

Make things predictable and natural to ensure they're usable.

"Nothing is stronger than habit."
—Publius Ovidius Naso (Ovid), poet

The Problem

Solutions end up being hard to use when customer expectations and design heuristics are not considered.

The Solution

Create experiences that are easily understood and complement customer expectations.

- Group functionality together. Make it easy to get to content and features. Apply Fitt's law, which states the time required to rapidly move to a target area is a function of the distance to the target and the size of the target. Place related functionality closer together.[140] Less-important items should be further away or remain hidden until required.

- Make it second nature. If it looks like it should work a certain way, it should. Understand what customers are used to, and create experiences that match expectations. Smartphone touch gestures let consumers navigate, interact, and entertain themselves naturally.[141]

- Be forgiving. Customers are human, so they will make mistakes. Design your features using a forgiving format that expects a degree of error.[142] Give users a chance to recover, often with some guidance, so they can proceed to complete tasks.

---

140. http://en.wikipedia.org/wiki/Fitts_law
141. http://www.zeldman.com/2010/04/20/touch-gesture-reference-guide/
142. http://ui-patterns.com/patterns/ForgivingFormat

Take a Walk

Get away from your desk to get the answers.

"Even a soul submerged in sleep is hard at work and helps make something of the world."
—Heraclitus, philosopher

The Problem

Teams forced to come up with inspirational ideas while having to consider risks and delivery pressures fail because they can't relax enough to let the creative juices flow.

The Solution

Step away from your desk and work environment. Inspiration will come when you don't focus too hard or too closely on the problem.

- Stop when you lose interest. Get remotivated. Remove barriers you are facing. Improve or learn a new skill. Then return to the problem better prepared to tackle it. Use BJ Fogg's behavior model to help you simplify problems you want to solve.[143]

- Interrupt yourself. Take regular breaks. Unfinished tasks remain in the subconscious part of your brain, which keeps working away at the problem even when you have consciously switched focus. This is known as the Zeigarnik effect.[144]

- Be happy. Use positive psychology and positive memory recall to freely attract related experiences and creative solutions. Events and emotions are linked, so relax to recall useful insights and memories from the past to help you solve your problems.[145]

---

143. http://www.behaviormodel.org/
144. http://www.psychwiki.com/wiki/Zeigarnik_Effect
145. http://www.ppc.sas.upenn.edu/

Celebrate Success

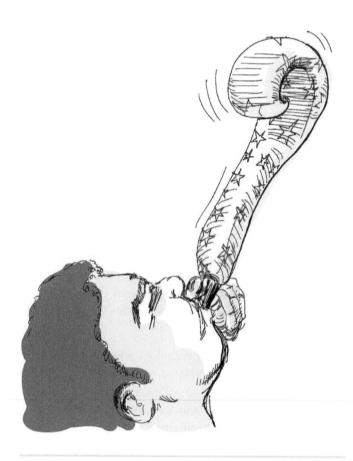

Thank people for their good work.

"Action is the foundational key to all success."
—Pablo Picasso, artist

The Problem

Employees leave because companies don't appreciate them.

The Solution

Recognize valuable contributions and reward employees accordingly.

- Cultivate a fun, creative work environment. Allow workers to enjoy themselves whenever they need a break from work. I have used Nerf Blasters, game consoles like the Microsoft Xbox and Nintendo Wii, and traditional sports such as table tennis to keep teams motivated through play.[146,147]

- Highlight success. Recognize outstanding employee contributions at award ceremonies or by mentioning them at daily and weekly meetings. Mention names in company newsletters and note details of good work in more-formal employee performance reviews.

- Thank customers too. Loyalty is hard to come by, so surprise those who have been customers for a while by giving them discounts on services, early previews of new releases, and real-world reward vouchers they can spend on the things they enjoy the most.

146. http://en.wikipedia.org/wiki/Nerf_Blasters
147. http://en.wikipedia.org/wiki/Play_(activity)

Part III

Ingredients to Help You Cross the Finish Line

Ingredient 56

Make It Personal

Understand why it matters to individuals.

"The will to win, the desire to succeed, the urge to reach your full potential…these are the keys that will unlock the door to personal excellence."
—Confucius, teacher, politician, and philosopher

The Problem

It's hard to earn people's trust, but easy to lose it. If employees don't see the benefits of giving you their time and energy, they won't bother.

The Solution

Match personal team-member and stakeholder needs fully and accurately.

- Show how it affects them. Don't assume people want the same things. Stakeholders have business metrics, developers want to try new techniques, designers want to win awards. The Wellbeing North Star innovation game gets project teams to share important personal requirements.[148]

- Give face-to-face feedback. Make team feedback and appraisals contextually relevant and actionable. Take into account the employee's perception of value. Make feedback personal, timely, and comfortable.[149]

- Let them track progress and help them solve specific problems. The Adidas miCoach mobile app lets sports coaches track their athletes' performance. Learn from this to track your team's performance too.[150]

---

148. http://innovationgames.com/wellbeing-north-star/
149. http://www.forbes.com/sites/meghanbiro/2013/01/13/5-ways-leaders-rock-employee-recognition/
150. http://www.springwise.com/lifestyle_leisure/trackers-embedded-athletes-apparel-provide-live-in-game-data-coaches/

Ingredient 57

Don't Get Distracted

Don't let anything get in your way.

"You can't depend on your eyes when your imagination is out of focus."
—Mark Twain, author and humorist

The Problem

Teams take longer to complete projects because they waste time working on things they didn't have to.

The Solution

Get your team to focus on the most important tasks.

- Agree on goals. Constantly check and realign project scope, roles, and responsibilities. Challenge unclear assumptions and requirements before prioritizing any work. Record changes so you can refer back to them at a later date.

- Say no. Avoid scope creep by pushing back on new requirements that make little sense. Only factor in relevant insight that results in the delivery of a better product. Don't reprioritize, stop, or change anything until you have validated the importance of an insight.

- Stay motivated.[151] Identify what each team member needs to complete tasks efficiently. Work to support each other, playing to individual strengths so everyone stays interested in delivering great results for the duration of the project.

---

151. http://www.sixsigmaonline.org/six-sigma-training-certification-information/
articles/light-the-fire---motivating-team-members-to-succeed-at-all-times.html

Ingredient 58

Stop Making It Up

Turning a graph upside down doesn't make it right.

"However beautiful the strategy, you should occasionally look at the results."
—Winston Churchill, prime minister of the United Kingdom, 1940–1945 and 1951–1955

The Problem

Teams develop ideas based on insufficient, incorrect, and biased requirements.

The Solution

Accept truth revealed through customer validation and usability testing.

- Validate assumptions. It is human nature to conjure up an explanation to make sense of things, even when there's no proof. This is known as cognitive dissonance.[152] Find concrete evidence instead to avoid heartache later.

- Stay open-minded. Don't let your strong points of view influence the truth. Be careful not to fall into the confirmation-bias trap.[153] Try to let the stats speak for themselves instead, and interpret them without bias.

- Don't lead. It's tempting to want to help customers during a usability test, for example, but this will taint the results. Let them make mistakes and experience things naturally without any external intervention to avoid the observer-expectancy effect.[154] Observe, take notes, and be prepared to take honest and insightful feedback.

---

152. http://psychcentral.com/blog/archives/2008/10/19/fighting-cognitive-disso-nance-the-lies-we-tell-ourselves/
153. http://youarenotsosmart.com/2010/06/23/confirmation-bias/
154. http://en.wikipedia.org/wiki/Observer-expectancy_effect

Ingredient 59

Surprise Them

Reveal something that surpasses desires and expectations.

"If you always do what you always do, you will always get what you always have."
—Voltaire (François-Marie Arouet), French Enlightenment writer, historian, and philosopher

The Problem

Stakeholder feedback can be damaging if the stakeholders don't have the right context to make useful suggestions.

The Solution

Involve stakeholders when it makes sense, and build up a good business case before you finally show them what you have come up with.

- Show how easily it fits. Show how your solution integrates comfortably with current brand, marketing, technology, and internal processes; make the adoption of your ideas as pain-free as possible.

- Emphasize business value. There is nothing better than showing stakeholders what they will get as a return on investment. Highlight how new ideas have improved the most-important business metrics so they have no doubt about backing you.

- Wow them. Match ease of integration and clear business benefits with a world-class user experience. Apple product launches have this one-two-three punch.[155] Go beyond expectations to really amaze stakeholders and customers. Aim to win awards and the hearts of many fans.

---

155. http://www.businessinsider.com/best-keynotes-by-steve-jobs-2011-8?op=1

Check the Data

People may be taking a break, not stumbling across a barrier.

"Not everything that can be counted counts, and not everything that counts can be counted."
—Albert Einstein, theoretical physicist

The Problem

Companies don't monitor customer usage closely enough to see what's really going on.

The Solution

Analyze and interpret data as part of the design and build process. Shed light on uncertainties, especially if you aren't sure why they really exist.

- Have assumptions to test. There is no point looking at data if you do not know what you are looking for to start with. List your biggest assumptions and measure success by seeing if they have led to improvements to key performance indicators or success metrics.[156]

- Monitor changes over time. Don't just take one random look. Continue to monitor performance each time you make an improvement, and track changes with groups of users. This is known as batch and cohort analysis.[157]

- Don't make things up. There is no such thing as random data—there is only data you have not interpreted yet. Get to the bottom of any unusual behavior and don't go for the obvious, unfounded answer just because it's easier to accept. You'd be succumbing to the false-consensus effect.[158]

---

156. http://www.ap-institute.com/Key%20Performance%20Indicators.html
157. http://www.ashmaurya.com/2010/07/3-rules-to-actionable-metrics/
158. http://www.spring.org.uk/2007/11/why-we-all-stink-as-intuitive.php

Ingredient 61

Adapt Quickly

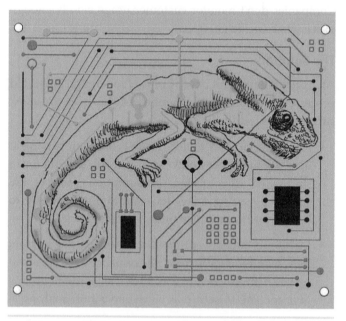

Adapt to your environment to capitalize on new trends.

"Those who cannot change their minds cannot change anything."
—George Bernard Shaw, playwright, and cofounder of the London School of Economics

The Problem

Companies take too long thinking about their next moves. By the time a decision is made, solutions are out of date and competitors have come up with something better.

The Solution

Speed up and be ready to make improvements based on research and analysis.

- Timebox your market research and requirements-gathering. Do just enough to get a feel for what customers are trending toward. Pitch the results to stakeholders, showing them the positive effect on the business, then get them to agree on an appropriate course of action. Prepare to make changes immediately.

- Start with a simple paper prototype and test early.[159] Once main ideas have proven to be successful, you can quickly move to a more robust and realistic prototype users can employ in the channel of their choice (mobile, laptop, interactive TV) to test more in-depth experiences.

- Run rapid iterative tests (RITEs) and take insights from each day to make important changes before testing again a few days later.[160] Do this three to five times in succession until you have something vastly improved based on real user feedback.

---

159. http://www.nngroup.com/reports/paper-prototyping-training-video/
160. http://uxtogo.wordpress.com/2012/03/23/rite-testing-is-about-team-engagement/

Ingredient 62

Find Allies

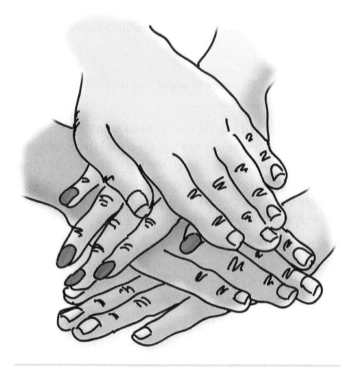

Find the right partner to deliver the right solution with you.

"Friendship is essentially a partnership."
—Aristotle, philosopher and teacher of Alexander the Great

The Problem

Companies try to do everything themselves, so end up wasting time and money producing substandard products.

The Solution

Work with people and teams to deliver your project and create a superior product more cost-effectively.

- Identify your weaknesses. Get coworkers, stakeholders, and the market to identify key areas and skills you need to improve. Partnerships between IT solution-providers and telecom agents are proving to be hugely successful for both parties involved.[161]

- Get the best. Source best-of-breed partners with proven track records. List their pros and cons before selecting one based on your prioritized needs. The Comcast and Intel partnership helps Intel better market its products and complements Comcast's efforts at expanding streaming services.[162]

- Hire the competition. Find the right key players, even if they are coming from a competitor. Don't come across as incapable, but be seen as focused and honest instead. Electrolux hired Stefano Marzano from Royal Philips Electronics to be the company's new chief design officer. Marzano brought expertise and fit in well with Electrolux's focus to get research and development, marketing, and design functions in synergy.[163] Be careful to know who your friends are, though.

---

161. http://blog.comptia.org/2012/07/31/telecom-it-partnerships-paying-off/
162. http://www.forbes.com/sites/greatspeculations/2013/01/17/comcast-intels-partnership-whats-at-stake-for-comcast/
163. http://group.electrolux.com/en/electrolux-appoints-stefano-marzano-to-the-new-role-of-chief-design-officer-12658/

Keep People Informed

Reduce the frustration of not knowing what to do next.

"The beginning of knowledge is the discovery of something we do not understand."
—Frank Herbert, author

The Problem

Anger, impatience, and fear increase when teams don't keep customers and stakeholders up-to-date.

The Solution

Have useful information at hand to back up what you're doing.

- Establish a cadence. Send out a weekly report and schedule review and showcase sessions.[164] Stress the need to fully understand what has been discussed or is required, and highlight the risks of people misinterpreting announcements or missing meetings. Increase the frequency of reports to force conversations between stakeholders. Over-communication is OK.

- Show progress. Make it easy to see what has been achieved, how much has been spent, and what is coming next—use a Kanban wall chart.[165] Walk through key decisions that have been made and what people can expect next.

- Interpret data. Set up project dashboards and let interested parties generate their own performance reports.[166] Use graphs and infographics to make it easier to digest important statistics. Include any bad news, as this is less upsetting than getting bad news out of the blue.

---

164. http://www.projectsmart.com/project-management/communicating-progress.php
165. http://www.kanbanblog.com/explained/index.html
166. http://mashable.com/2012/04/23/website-analytics-dashboard-tools/

Ingredient 64

Don't Show Up

Avoid meetings that aren't important.

"Meetings are indispensable when you don't want to do anything."
—John Kenneth Galbraith, economist

The Problem

People waste time going to meetings when they're better off doing productive work instead.

The Solution

Only attend meetings for clarification and to keep you moving forward.

- Say no. Don't think you can do everything and underestimate the time it takes to attend meetings. Decline ones with no clear agenda or objective. Learn to turn people away if something more important warrants your time. Choose one thing to focus on at a time.[167]

- Be busy. Book time in your calendar for yourself to complete important work. Show yourself as out of office and busy so no one can disturb you. Get meeting organizers to justify prioritizing their meeting over your work. Challenge the agenda.[168] If it's not important they will reschedule.

- Demonstrate a better way.[169] Send a proxy. Make a decision over email. Cut down meeting times and keep the number of attendees small. Reduce the amount of process and effort involved.

---

167. http://www.inc.com/ilya-pozin/get-your-focus-back-7-tips.html
168. http://www.inc.com/kevin-daum/3-ways-to-keep-meetings-short-every-time.html
169. http://www.fastcodesign.com/1669936/meetings-are-a-skill-you-can-master-and-steve-jobs-taught-me-how

Don't Think Too Much

Avoid analysis paralysis.

"Everybody gets so much information all day long that they lose their common sense."
—Gertrude Stein, art collector and writer

The Problem

Companies spend too much time researching, leaving teams little time to do the work.

The Solution

Do just enough to get going. Make decisions based on reality rather than theory alone.

- Make a start. Come up with ideas that match business needs together with stakeholders and your team. Do enough research and competitor analysis, and put them into a prioritized list of features using a discovery process that can get you going quickly, leaving you more time to make changes later.[170]

- Test and learn.[171] Create the lowest-fidelity prototypes you can get away with to validate those big assumptions. Employ lean-user-experience methods to test assumptions and gauge success through experimentation.[172] Gain insight and improve your ideas iteratively.

- Keep it real-time. Analyze real-time interactions and use the insight to make improvements so you can still meet agreed-upon business success metrics. Use a tool like Google Analytics to generate specific reports that will help you analyze the data you have about your online presence.[173]

---

170. http://www.sitepoint.com/9-tips-for-a-successful-discovery-process/

171. http://www.gilliganondata.com/index.php/2012/07/31/a-pragmatic-approach-to-test-and-learn/

172. http://uxdesign.smashingmagazine.com/2011/03/07/lean-ux-getting-out-of-the-deliverables-business/

173. http://www.smashingmagazine.com/2009/07/16/a-guide-to-google-analytics-and-useful-tools/

Make It Interesting

Stand out and be remembered.

"My interest is in the future because I am going to spend the rest of my life there."
—Charles Kettering, inventor

The Problem

Companies can't differentiate themselves from competitors, so they don't leave a lasting impression with customers.

The Solution

Connect with customers in a memorable way your competitors haven't yet been able to.

- Fit in. Make your products and services emotionally interesting.[174] Use mood-driven advertising, give passionate talks, and engage people through social networks. Customers want relationships with brands that match their beliefs, but through their preferred channels.

- Be easy to remember. Focus your efforts in one area and show how you are better than a competitor. Don't do too many things, as this will add confusion and make customers remember you for the wrong reasons. Do less to do more.[175]

- Delight and surprise.[176] Reveal new and useful features regularly. Track customer issues and feedback to decide what to improve, and really wow them. Aim to remain fresh and attractive to new and existing customers.

---

174. http://www.communicoltd.com/pages/1076_four_key_strategies_for_building_emotional_connections_with_your_customers.cfm

175. http://www.forbes.com/sites/jeffbercovici/2012/04/17/yahoo-ceos-turnaround-plan-do-less-do-it-better/

176. http://www.clickz.asia/7018/creating_brand_advocacy_through_surprise_and_delight_moments

Make It Accessible

Let people experience it how they want.

"There is a single light of science, and to brighten it anywhere is to brighten it everywhere."
—Isaac Asimov, author and professor of biochemistry

The Problem

Most companies do not understand how, when, and where customers engage, which leads to experiences that are fragmented, unusable, and inconsistent.

The Solution

Make your products and services available to as many people as possible without sacrificing quality.

- Comply. Understand and meet guideline recommendations to reach the maximum number of customers possible. Organizations like the W3C define global guidelines that companies like the BBC adapt to meet their own online accessibility needs.[177,178]

- Match expectations. Understand what situations and environments customers experience the most when engaging with your company or idea. Gain insight through market research, customer interviews, focus groups, and data analytics to spot and fix areas where they struggle the most.

- Simplify and forgive. Put in extra time to test and streamline the user interface and interactions across multiple devices and customer touchpoints. Try incorporating a responsive web design—a great way to ensure that experiences for different screen resolutions and platforms automatically readjust based on one single code base.[179]

177. http://www.w3.org/WAI/
178. http://www.bbc.co.uk/guidelines/futuremedia/accessibility/
179. http://mashable.com/2012/12/11/responsive-web-design/

Ingredient 68

Tell a Good Story

Let team members play a part in defining the experience.

"Words without thoughts never to heaven go."
—William Shakespeare, poet and playwright

The Problem

If a project doesn't sound interesting, chances are the end delivery will be a mediocre one.

The Solution

Get team members excited about the difference they can make on a project and the rewards that will be gained when it's delivered.

- Let your team shine. Empower your team to come up with ways to deliver something amazing. Show how customers will benefit from parts of the project or service they have worked on personally and how it is much better than the competition.

- Meet both customer and business needs.[180] Leverage relevant market opportunities, customer trends, and usage analytics to gain the insight you need to justify how new features and functionality meet customer needs while producing a good return on investment.

- Help your marketing and sales team highlight the right benefits when promoting your big idea, and give customers, partners, and stakeholders an exciting story to tell to their peers and bosses.[181] If you don't, they will only make it up themselves.

---

180. http://blogs.sas.com/content/sascom/2011/08/13/how-to-meet-business-needs-and-user-needs-with-bi/

181. http://www.smashingmagazine.com/2010/07/20/yin-and-yang-oil-and-water-creative-and-marketing/

Ingredient 69

Reward Them

Feed them if that's what keeps them going.

"No person is honored for what he receives. Instead, honor is the reward for what they gave."
—Calvin Coolidge, 30th president of the United States

The Problem

Keeping team members happy so they continue to perform well is difficult even if your intentions are good.

The Solution

Understand your team's motivations and capabilities. Reward them for doing a good job with what really matters to them.

- Create a rewards system. Agree on the rewards teams can expect when they deliver the goods. This can be a bonus, a team outing, or time off. Whatever it is, make sure it is something they want. This matching of expectations is known as positive reinforcement.[182]

- Help them overcome barriers. BJ Fogg's behavior model identifies psychological barriers affecting a team's performance. Give your team the skills and training to tackle tasks more effectively.[183]

- Encourage healthy competition. Teams can use a project's dashboard to keep track of what the team has achieved and how it has performed compared to other teams. Encourage team members to discuss, share knowledge, and reward each other (peer-to-peer rewards). Zappos employees can give each other Zollars for any action that they feel is deserving of recognition, for example.[184]

---

182. http://en.wikipedia.org/wiki/Reward_system
183. http://www.behaviormodel.org/
184. http://www.zapposinsights.com/about/faqs#q22

Keep It Under the Radar

Don't show anyone until you can prove a point.

"Secret operations are essential in war; upon them the army relies to make its every move."
—Sun Tzu, military general, strategist, and philosopher

The Problem

Great ideas are diluted when shown too early to stakeholders who want something more predictable.

The Solution

Keep your idea under wraps and continue to prove customer and business value until your brave concept sees the light of day.

- Find time. Get the time to work on something you feel passionate about. Forward-thinking companies allow employees to work on projects that they choose. Find a project that interests both you and your company so you get the right amount of time and support to see it through.

- Don't invite stakeholders. Involve them only to make strategic decisions; give them little chance to interfere with creative direction or technology questions except at key review stages. Understand the business strategy so you can factor that into design or technology solutions you provide.

- Experiment and analyze. Create prototypes to test your idea. Use key data metrics to prove your idea is the best option. People will be willing to "unlearn" and adopt new approaches and solutions if you back them up with solid analytical results.

Ingredient 71

Have an Opinion

Stand up for your beliefs, and people will take notice.

"Everything we hear is an opinion, not a fact. Everything we see is a perspective, not the truth."
—Marcus Aurelius, Roman emperor and philosopher

The Problem

If it's not clear what you stand for, people will find it hard to differentiate you from what others have to offer.

The Solution

Take a stand about something customers and stakeholders care about. Help them identify with your beliefs by proving what you have is what they need.

- Spread your vision. Write statements and papers, give talks and demos, speak to other thought leaders. Promote what you believe in all the time.

- Give examples. Gain people's support by showing relevant examples of how your beliefs have been applied to address similar problems and needs. Use case studies and personal experiences to show that what you are talking about has worked before.

- Prove it works for them. Create a bespoke demonstration and prototype, based on your beliefs, that solves a specific problem for them. Back it up with real customer validation so there is no doubt it works.

Be Good

It takes only one bad experience for people to lose all faith.

"Always do right—this will gratify some and astonish the rest."
—Mark Twain, author and humorist

The Problem

A bad experience lasts much longer than a good one, making it very hard to regain customer trust when companies do something wrong.

The Solution

Give customers more reasons to feel good about using your products.

- Get the basics right. Understand customer expectations and apply best practices to functionality that should work as a given. This will persuade customers that you know what you are doing and make them more comfortable engaging in more-complex requirements further down the line.

- Look after customers. Don't make them do more than they need to achieve success or get a response. Reassure customers and help them complete tasks and keep track of any progress made. Make it easy for them to get answers when they need them.

- Associate with good. Make parting with money more acceptable by giving some of it to charity, awarding cash back, or building up rewards customers can spend on products and services they really care about.

Ingredient 73

Cut through the Bull

Focus on what matters to see if arguments still hold true.

"The truth is more important than the facts."
—Frank Lloyd Wright, architect

The Problem

Teams rely on outdated processes and techniques to meet new requirements, so they never fully address important issues on time.

The Solution

Do a reality check and demonstrate better ways to achieve success so you can update existing processes and finally get things done.

- Challenge the status quo. Question the need to stick to protocol by highlighting weaknesses in existing processes and tools. Identify and agree on the key objectives as a team and a business to see if existing ways are still effective.

- Find alternatives. Do your research and find up-to-date alternatives. Get expert peer recommendations and refer to industry advice, including best practices. Compare the benefits of new and existing approaches. Show your team and other relevant stakeholders how easy it will be to make any changes.

- Reinforce any learning. Make it clear and easy to remember key benefits compared to what exists today. Use qualitative as well as quantitative facts and figures to help you come across more convincingly, but be careful not to overload your team with too much information at once.

Ingredient 74

Make It Emotional

Eurostar planned to spend hundreds of millions to reduce travel time from London to Paris by 15 minutes. Free Wi-Fi would have cost considerably less and made the commute more delightful.

"Some men look at things the way they are and ask why. I dream of things that are not and ask why not."
—Robert Kennedy, United States senator

The Problem

Solving immediate problems stops companies from noticing what people really care about.

The Solution

Understand what customers value most to improve experiences they will actually appreciate.

- Appeal to multiple senses to reinforce your idea. Think about modalities, location, intensity, and duration of the stimulus, also known as multimodal integration.[185] Coffee shops use the smell of fresh coffee and the sound of coffee being ground to intensify and extend the experience.

- Don't anchor solutions on what's rational.[186] Psychological decisions that are driven by spreadsheets and return-on-investment feasibility tend not to be in the interest of the customer.

- Be more creative. Tap into your emotional intelligence to solve problems more effectively. Observe what people do and feel to arrive at a solution that's simple and hits the mark.[187]

---

185. http://www.beyondcurrenthorizons.org.uk/knowledge-creativity-and-communication-in-education-multimodal-design/
186. http://persuasive-patterns.com/patterns/Anchoring
187. http://psychology.about.com/od/personalitydevelopment/a/emotionalintell.htm

Ingredient 75

Build Up Enough Momentum

Fine-tune ideas until they can spring to life.

"Small opportunities are often the beginning of great enterprises."
—Demosthenes, politician

The Problem

Organizations launch substandard products because they have hard deadlines to meet.

The Solution

Starting with a minimum viable product, continually fine-tune your idea until it's ready to be launched.

- Keep the fire burning.[188] Work on ideas you're passionate about and remember your vested interest in solving the problem. Want to make a difference and stay focused.

- React to changing market and customer trends.[189] Time your launch to coincide with important shifts and events that affect your product. Weigh the risks to see if your idea will be strong enough if changes don't work in your favor.

- Go small. Don't overpromise and underdeliver. Be ready with an idea that is basic but hard to duplicate. Focus all your energy on perfecting simplicity and matching what your product does with important customer needs.

---

188. http://www.haironfirepm.com/2012/12/12/is-your-persistence-and-passion-affecting-your-project-team/
189. http://www.inc.com/encyclopedia/market-research_pagen_2.html

Create a Tipping Point

Keep pushing ahead with your idea until it snowballs.

"You cannot push anyone up the ladder unless he is willing to climb."
—Andrew Carnegie, industrialist

The Problem

Companies focus their efforts on getting something launched and don't work with customers to evolve it into something amazing.

The Solution

Leave enough time after launching an idea to market it, leaning on social connectors, mavens, and salesmen to help spread the word. Aim to reach what Malcolm Gladwell calls the tipping point.[190]

- Fill a gap. Conduct market research to see what exists today. Decide how your idea can succeed where others may have failed. Put together a business model and plan, including costs, time scales, competitor analysis, and benefits to sell your idea to stakeholders convincingly.

- Be passionate but flexible. Enthuse team members and stakeholders, but also set realistic expectations and highlight risks. Show you are prepared to do whatever it takes to test the idea in the market, but be prepared to adapt based on available time, technology, resources, and business priorities.

- Keep moving forward. Respond to customer feedback and observed behaviors by creating missing functionality, improving existing functionality, and removing any obstacles. Track every improvement to check that nothing breaks and that the holistic customer journey is still optimized.

---

190. http://en.wikipedia.org/wiki/The_Tipping_Point

Execute It Well

The beginning, middle, and end are all important.

"To affect the quality of the day, that is the highest of arts."
—Henry David Thoreau, author, poet, and philosopher

The Problem

Companies that don't appreciate good design produce products and services that people won't cherish.

The Solution

Focus on delivering a quality experience where design is factored in throughout the product-development process.

- First impressions count, so make them good. Apple has a dedicated person who opens its product boxes behind the scenes to ensure the first-time out-of-the-box customer experience is brilliant.[191] Customers are thanked with a wonderful unveiling that oozes care and quality even before they've turned on the device they have purchased.

- Make it usable. The Xerox Star was the first graphical user interface (GUI),[192] but not until Apple got its hands on the GUI to improve the customer experience did it became something personal-computer users could actually use.

- Check that it works everywhere. Design your product to work on any device.[193] Factor in cross-browser testing and implement a responsive design framework so your service can work on multiple devices, including web, mobile, and interactive TV.

191. http://www.gizmodo.co.uk/2012/01/apple-packing-is-so-good-because-they-employ-a-dedicated-box-opener/
192. http://en.wikipedia.org/wiki/Xerox_Star
193. http://coding.smashingmagazine.com/2011/01/12/guidelines-for-responsive-web-design/

Part IV

Ingredients to Get More of What You Want

Ingredient 78

Look Outside to Be More Effective

Look out the window to see what's really going on.

"Every man takes the limits of his own field of vision for the limits of the world."
—Arthur Schopenhauer, philosopher

The Problem

Companies don't factor in trends outside of their core focus that could make them more successful.

The Solution

Understand wider market and customer trends to leverage interesting insight.

- Know what's hot. Subscribe to a trend-spotting service (for example, Trend Watching), review popular technology blogs (for example, Mashable), and absorb industry news (from sites such as TechCrunch) to gain insight and identify trends that may fit with your company's vision and values.[194,195,196]

- Try something new. Experiment with new technologies, processes, and ideas that can improve what you deliver and how you deliver. Get feedback from early adopters and run development spikes to help you decide how to spend your time and money.[197,198]

- Network with experts. Attend industry events, talk to peers, and partner up with anyone who can help your team do a better job. Lanyrd is a useful tool for identifying technology events around the world that you and your peers can attend to stay ahead of the game.[199]

---

194. http://www.trendwatching.com/
195. http://mashable.com/
196. http://techcrunch.com/
197. http://www.wired.com/gadgetlab/2011/11/9-gadgets-that-prove-youre-a-hard-core-early-adopter/
198. http://agile.dzone.com/news/development-spikes-technical
199. http://lanyrd.com/

Ingredient 79

Do It Because You Can't

Innovative ideas are ones no one thought possible.

"Start by doing what's necessary; then do what's possible; and suddenly you are doing the impossible."
—Francis of Assisi, Catholic friar and preacher

The Problem

Teams and businesses give up when an idea gets too hard to handle.

The Solution

Work on that idea people say can't be done. It could just be because no one's found a way yet.

- Analyze failed attempts. Interview customers and stakeholders to find out why something didn't work. Next, assess current market conditions for new or renewed interest before formulating an approach to give it another go. The early days of Yahoo!'s attempt to become the largest social network taught Facebook to avoid the mistakes of failing to grow and to maintain a large online community.[200]

- Get them to love it. Enthuse your team by showing them the benefits of completing a project no one thinks is possible. Hire people who are hungry and capable—people who share your passion.[201]

- Start simple. Do whatever it takes to prove that the experience is what customers want.[202] Get people to understand the benefits and incrementally build on each successful and failed validation. Put your idea in front of customers and show stakeholders the progress your team is making.

200. http://www.forbes.com/sites/davidcooperstein/2012/06/05/how-facebook-can-avoid-being-the-next-yahoo/
201. http://mashable.com/2008/07/29/building-your-startup-team/
202. http://unbounce.com/101-landing-page-optimization-tips/

Cast It Far, Then Reel It In

Go that little bit further than everyone else.

"I like the dreams of the future better than the history of the past."
—Thomas Jefferson, US Founding Father

The Problem

Companies and teams aren't good at making radical changes to their own products even when they know what is possible and what should be done.

The Solution

Find a way to look further afield; identify and execute opportunities no one else can see. If you reach for the moon and fall short, you will still achieve something amazing.

- Create a vision of the future. Microsoft creates and films proof-of-concept Future Vision videos to show the world what the company plans to achieve in the next ten to fifteen years.[203] Aim high to define the outer limits of what the world can have, then create a strategy to articulate this vision.

- Plan for the future. Differentiate between long-term, secular trends like cloud computing, and cyclical trends like social networks, which need to be factored in today for more personalized products and services. *Secular* growth reflects an expansion of a market that happens once in a lifetime.[204] If you gain some unique insight into the future, grab it with both hands and be ready to do something about it as soon as possible.

- Separate innovation. There is a difference between disruptive and continuous innovation. Set aside time to work on new game-changing ideas, separate from making improvements to existing functionality. Red Gate Software has a Down Tools Week every three months, when employees set aside their day-to-day tasks and work on their own projects.[205]

---

203. http://youtu.be/8Ff7SzP4gfg
204. http://washingtontechnology.com/articles/2013/02/19/chao-govcon-innovation.aspx
205. http://ux.red-gate.com/computer-says-no-a-down-tools-project

Ingredient 81

Be Unreasonable

Why not be perfect if you can?

"The reasonable man adapts himself to the world. The unreasonable man adapts the world to himself. All progress depends on the unreasonable man."
—George Bernard Shaw, playwright, and cofounder of the London School of Economics

The Problem

Companies don't offer enough value to customers, so they achieve little growth.

The Solution

Push the limits. Believe you can change the world and set out to do it.

- Be ignorant. Too much knowledge makes teams and businesses play it too safe. Under certain conditions newcomers can produce innovation in areas they are exposed to. Use your ignorance of a particular subject or industry to come up with ideas; apply the "newcomer effect" to your advantage.[206]

- Make a fool of yourself. It may not make much sense yet, but if your research proves there's an opportunity, give it a go. Don't worry if people laugh, criticize, or put you down. Steve Jobs's address to Stanford University students encouraging them to "Stay hungry, stay foolish" sums it all up.[207] Don't let opportunities to change the world pass you by.

- Reach for the skies. Go above and beyond to create experiences that wow customers and make stakeholders want to invest more time and money with you.[208]

---

206. http://d-scholarship.pitt.edu/9128/
207. http://www.youtube.com/watch?v=D1R-jKKp3NA
208. http://www.forbes.com/sites/avidan/2013/01/14/writing-an-awesome-letter-to-a-7-year-old-and-gaining-a-lifetime-customer-for-lego/

Ingredient 82

Crowdsource It

Let people help each other.

"We must learn to live together as brothers or perish together as fools."
—Martin Luther King, Jr., clergyman, activist, and leader in the African-American civil-rights movement

The Problem

Companies don't listen to what the majority of customers say or want, so they end up delivering experiences that don't really matter.

The Solution

Let customers define what's right. Act on inputs that make the most sense, and recognize the hard work being done for you.

- Allow collaboration. Wikipedia lets knowledge experts create, input, and evolve encyclopedia definitions. This interactive evolutionary computation, working as a team of global experts, ensures a high level of quality and relevancy.[209,210]

- Highlight similarity. Let people review and rate content to help others with similar needs find useful and interesting content. Amazon was the first online shopping website to recommend what shoppers might like based on what others found interesting.[211]

- Encourage advocacy. Passionate customers who love your products and services will naturally spread the word via their social and professional networks.[212] Reward those who help you reach more customers by letting them test new ideas before anyone else.

---

209. http://www.wikipedia.org/
210. http://en.wikipedia.org/wiki/Interactive_evolutionary_computation
211. http://www.amazon.com
212. http://mashable.com/2011/03/18/social-media-consumer-advocacy/

Ingredient 83

Don't Do It All

A jack-of-all-trades is a master of none.

"The man who promises everything is sure to fulfill nothing."
—Carl Jung, psychotherapist and psychiatrist who founded analytical psychology

The Problem

Companies who try to please everyone end up with solutions that don't do anything well.

The Solution

Focus on improving the quality, accuracy, and usability of fewer features to keep customers happy and help your organization remain competitive.

- Identify what's important. Assess customer, business, and competitor impact. Don't forget to factor in any crucial dependencies. Agree on a core set of features with your team and stakeholders. This will become your minimum viable product.[213]

- Partner up.[214] Identify features that are important but not within your delivery capabilities. Find an internal or external resource who has the skills you require, and work closely with that resource to deliver these features.

- Confirm relevancy. See if your original assumptions still hold true. Factor in up-to-date market changes and adapt your road map accordingly to incorporate new useful insight.

---

213. http://en.wikipedia.org/wiki/Minimum_viable_product
214. http://www.cio.com/article/127152/Collaborative_Innova-
    tion_Five_Steps_to_Successful_Technology_Partnerships

Ingredient 84

Stay Hungry, Stay Foolish

Never give up. Keep believing until it works.

"Whether you think that you can or that you can't, you are usually right."
—Henry Ford, founder of the Ford Motor Company

The Problem

Companies and teams aren't compelled to innovate when they don't need to. They don't take risks for fear of rocking the boat.

The Solution

Believe you can do it. Innovative ideas come about when teams take a chance and are committed to never give up until their idea becomes a reality.

- Stop making excuses. When you really want something, you will find a way—using any means necessary. Pull in favors, stop getting distracted; keep moving and get closer to realizing your dreams.

- Adopt early.[215] Try new, unproven technology and approaches if they will help you realize ideas more easily. Do just enough research to get a prototype into the market, and keep evolving it until it becomes something wonderful.

- Make it personal. Invest your own blood, sweat, and tears to show how much you believe in an idea.[216] Others will notice this commitment and want to help you succeed.

---

215. http://www.techrepublic.com/blog/smbit/five-signs-that-being-an-early-technology-adopter-is-a-good-bet-for-your-business/201

216. http://www.forbes.com/sites/martinzwilling/2012/09/21/how-to-invest-in-startups-to-balance-your-portfolio/

Ingredient 85

Be Childish

Nothing's impossible when seen through innocent eyes.

"It is easier to build strong children than to repair broken men."
—Frederick Douglass, social reformer

The Problem

People have lost their ability to wonder, and don't allow failure to teach them valuable lessons.

The Solution

Recapture all that was positive, amazing, and fun as a child.[217] Regress and find new ways to achieve what you want without putting up unnecessary barriers.

- Be a superhero. Remember pretending to be Captain Spock or Luke Skywalker?[218] Role-play situations to come up with cool ideas and make them a reality. Become who you've always wanted to be.

- Be a know-it-all. Keep learning like a child. Children's brains are like sponges; they never stop learning. Give yourself the ammunition to counterargue and build strong business cases for your latest ideas. Children can be annoying, but only because they know more than adults.[219]

- Know what you want. Be ready to adopt new beliefs based on relevant evidence—whatever makes the most sense. Stay up-to-date with the latest trends. Children are always trying to understand each other and the world around them. "Babies and young children are like the R and D division of the human species," says psychologist Alison Gopnik.[220]

---

217. http://tinybuddha.com/blog/33-ways-to-be-childlike-today/
218. http://www.dailymail.co.uk/sciencetech/article-2221363/Google-reveals-Star-Trek-inspired-vision-future-computing.html
219. http://www.skyoneonline.co.uk/are_you_smarter/
220. http://www.ted.com/talks/alison_gopnik_what_do_babies_think.html

Get Bored Easily

Be the first to recognize it isn't good enough.

"Perhaps the world's second worst crime is boredom. The first is being a bore."
—Jean Baudrillard, sociologist and philosopher

The Problem

Companies go bust when they rest on their laurels and think they can drag out the existence of a substandard product.

The Solution

Raise the quality bar within your team and commit to continually raising it.

- Have thin skin. Be allergic to poor design execution. Refer back to your missions, objectives, and design principles.[221] Link quality to measurable metrics to track each successive improvement. Keep improving what isn't good enough.

- Give a damn. If it shows that you've spent time perfecting your product, people will choose you over a competitor. Perfectionism plays a crucial role in Apple's success. Apple products feel like blood, sweat, and tears have been spilt making them so beautiful.[222] Focus on the details.

- Let your mind wander. Be constantly on the lookout for a better way of doing things. Successful customer brand loyalty is based on the ability to continually delight.[223] Make sure to deliver incredible experiences across important delivery channels at every opportunity.

---

221. https://www.vitsoe.com/gb/about/good-design
222. http://www.newyorker.com/talk/financial/2011/10/17/
     111017ta_talk_surowiecki
223. http://www.forbes.com/sites/marketshare/2013/01/07/is-brand-loyalty-dying-
     a-slow-and-painful-death/

Don't Expect the Same Results

Try something new.

"Only the wisest and stupidest of men never change."
—Confucius, teacher, politician, and philosopher

The Problem

Companies apply the same fixed set of methods to different problems and pray for a good result.

The Solution

Approach each new idea with fresh eyes and avoid the pitfalls of economies of scale.[224] Explore better and more-appropriate ways to create what you need in a way that works.

- Avoid the scaling fallacy.[225] Verify load assumptions by testing and putting in place appropriate safety factors. Minimize incorrect scaling assumptions by carefully researching similar designs and monitoring how your idea performs post-implementation.

- Put them in the wild. Test subject-matter experts on real projects to assess how well they perform. Never assume that just because they're great in one situation they'll be great in an unrelated one. This unproven-expectation effect, known as the halo effect,[226] needs to be tested as quickly as possible.

- Change with the times. Try new technology and incorporate the latest market and customer trends. Don't be complacent and foolish, thinking you can keep doing what you are doing and continue to be successful. Learn from expert conferences, user groups, and online discussions, and take part in trials to stay ahead of the curve.

---

224. http://en.wikipedia.org/wiki/Economies_of_scale
225. http://embots.dfki.de/doc/seminar_ss09/ScalingFallacy.pdf
226. http://www.economist.com/node/14299211

Ingredient 88

Challenge and Disrupt

Keep asking why.

"There is nothing more difficult to take in hand, more perilous to conduct, or more uncertain in its success, than to take the lead in the introduction of a new order of things."
—Niccolo Machiavelli, historian and politician

The Problem

Out-of-date points of view, processes, and rules can't be used to solve current or future business needs.

The Solution

Highlight benefits of any new approach and help people adopt them as easily as possible.

- Question the status quo.[227] Challenge anything that no longer makes sense to remain the same. Use up-to-date business needs to suggest better, more-rewarding solutions.

- Prove it works.[228] Give examples of where a new approach has been successfully implemented by other teams and companies. Show how your team can create their own success stories.

- Make change easy.[229] Provide support to make changes as painless as possible. Organize training, refer to self-help tutorials, and have experts answer questions. Show how a small investment up-front will yield large returns in the near future.

---

227. http://www.lollydaskal.com/leadership/leadership-challenging-the-status-quo/
228. http://www.brw.com.au/p/sections/features/lean_start_up_thinking_for_big_fat_14AHWb2GQFaJLRm3KE6Dal
229. http://tinyurl.com/axt6hdx

Let Processes Form Around Needs

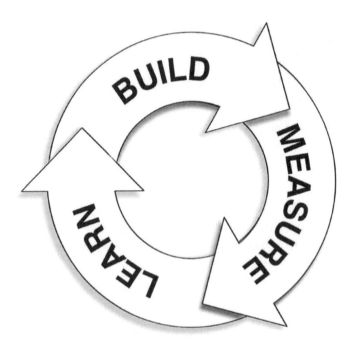

Find a better, more natural way of doing things.

"We do not learn; and what we call learning is only a process of recollection."
—Plato, mathematician and philosopher

The Problem

Companies shoehorn in processes that are out of date, out of context, and out of touch with reality.

The Solution

Create processes that match important criteria and conditions to improve workflow and maximize team efficiency.

- Evaluate existing processes. Look at the end goal and assess whether existing processes can achieve it efficiently. Highlight any failures, implement changes, and test the improved process on a small project. Fine-tune it until it represents a vast improvement over its predecessor.

- Adapt and combine. Often individual processes have feature duplication or unoptimized subprocesses. Take existing processes, remove any redundancy, identify the best parts of each, and combine them to create a streamlined one. For example, the evolution of the M25 Orbital Road in London, England, circumvented unnecessary routes to create fewer simpler ones.[230]

- Start from scratch. Create something that has never been done before to help you achieve your goals. The agile manifesto and lean-startup methodology are two disruptive examples of processes enabling organizations and teams to reduce documentation and wasteful development time.[231,232]

---

230. http://motorwayarchive.ihtservices.co.uk/en/motorways/motorway-listing/m25-london-orbital-motorway/origins-of-the-m25.cfm
231. http://agilemanifesto.org/
232. http://theleanstartup.com/

Increase Happiness

Smile to make everything better.

"Anything you're good at contributes to happiness."
—Bertrand Russell, philosopher, mathematician, and historian

The Problem

Unhappy people will be uncreative and unwilling to do anything useful.

The Solution

Get your team members to enjoy what they do. Martin Seligman, positive psychologist,[233] believes the happier we are the more successful we are.

- Reward your team with worldly pleasures. The pleasant life is the most visible measurement of happiness. Thank them by giving them bonuses, salary increases, time off, or a party. Although the shallowest of all types of happiness, the pleasant life is still sought after for its instant gratification.

- Help them maximize their potential to grow professionally. Enable individual team members to become subject-matter experts. Mentor, train, and expose them to opportunities to help them grow naturally to become recognized leaders in a field of expertise.

- Promote selflessness and living a meaningful life.[234] Encourage employees to help those in need by finding personal or client projects that improve the greater good—for example, charity work or speaking at educational institutions.

---

233. http://www.ppc.sas.upenn.edu/
234. http://en.wikipedia.org/wiki/Positive_psychology

Ingredient 91

Become an Expert

Be the headline act.

"The only real failure in life is not to be true to the best one knows."
—Buddha, founder of the Buddhist religion

The Problem

It's hard to promote a product or service if there's little prior proof of success.

The Solution

Prove you've been through battles and lived to tell the tales. People want to work with people who can achieve success for them easily and professionally.

- Teach. Explain how it all works. Use case studies and live demos, and reveal those amazing stories of success and failure. Make your presentations, workshops, and training sessions interesting, faultless, and professional so there's no doubt you know what you are talking about.

- Mentor. Help others better understand the theory by running workshops and training sessions. Take those interested through the process of creation, putting into practice what you have taught them. Let them experience, firsthand, what they have only ever heard or read about before.

- Be reliable. Reduce uncertainty and undesired consequences by defining solutions and advice that have been proven to work in similar situations. Do this time and time again. Soon they will realize the positive consequences of your involvement.

Ingredient 92

Know When to Give Up

Assess the damage around you before it's too late.

"The most interesting information comes from children, for they tell all they know and then stop."
—Mark Twain, author and humorist

The Problem

Companies don't stop projects that fail until too much time and effort has already been invested.

The Solution

Decide if implementing further improvements will make a difference. Assess the current situation and refocus your efforts on what's still relevant.

- Check that assumptions still hold true.[235] Set up regular stakeholder meetings to confirm that business needs are still the same. Refer to real customer data to support decisions. Improve assumptions that hold true, evolve ones that have potential, and stop those that prove false.

- Measure success.[236] For example, measure the increase in conversion rate and reduction in query resolution time. Monitor these metrics and stop the project if there is a prolonged downward trend, and find a better way to achieve success.

- Give it some time. Work in small batches to avoid the sunk-cost fallacy.[237] Don't pull the plug until you have done the minimum to market your product and attract your target customers. Remember that the innovation adoption curve has innovators and early adopters converting before the majority.[238] Focus on the majority, as that's where you want to attract loyal customers.

235. http://www.startup-marketing.com/wasting-time-validating-assumptions/
236. http://www.juiceanalytics.com/writing/5-rules-for-successful-success-metrics/
237. http://www.newyorker.com/talk/financial/2013/01/21/ 130121ta_talk_surowiecki
238. http://www.valuebasedmanagement.net/methods_rogers_innovation_adop- tion_curve.html

Ingredient 93

Don't Get Lazy

Be aware of important changes in your market.

"Inspiration is a guest that does not willingly visit the lazy."
—Pyotr Ilyich Tchaikovsky, composer

The Problem

Success lulls companies into a false sense of security, and teams become slow to react when they aren't actively being engaged.

The Solution

Allocate time to improve your skills and fine-tune your intuition.

- Get a mentor. Find someone to coach you and push you to your limits; improve existing skills, learn new ones, and become stronger as a team. Storify, for example, hired Don Loeb as its new business manager to retrain and inject startup success methodologies into its sales division.[239]

- Do your homework. Research relevant up-to-date market trends and attend talks and workshops about the hottest topics. Before you decide what to focus on, work with a trend-spotting company such as trendwatching.com to know how consumers are looking to spend their time and money.[240]

- Take risks while you can. Allocate time off projects to experiment with new approaches, software, and partnerships. Don't be afraid to fail; now is the time to figure out what is worth pursuing. Companies like Google allow up to twenty percent of work time to tinker and play.[241]

---

239. http://thenextweb.com/insider/2013/01/08/storify-hires-don-loeb-to-help-business-development/?fromcat=all
240. http://www.trendwatching.com/
241. http://www.wired.com/business/2012/12/llinkedin-20-percent-time/

Don't Jump to Conclusions

Don't conclude it's not there just because you can't see it.

"Death is the only pure, beautiful conclusion of a great passion."
—David Herbert Lawrence, novelist, poet, and playwright

The Problem

Overconfident companies who put all their eggs in one basket lose everything when expectations aren't met.

The Solution

Monitor ideas over time to see if they remain relevant.

- Dig deeper. Uncover the whole story. Investigate inconsistencies and unanswered questions. There may be less-obvious reasons why things aren't working. Use interesting insights to provide a better service than what exists today. Airbnb disrupted the hotel industry by allowing travelers to find cheaper accommodations hosted by local residents in their own homes.[242] Just because it's cheaper, that doesn't mean it's bad.

- Push past early adoption.[243] Don't assume early success via innovators and early adopters is an indicator of continued success. Keep raising awareness using a customer-growth plan to attract customers to your service.[244] Once they're there, maintain their interest by helping them make full use of features.

- Pivot. Validate ideas with customers to see if you're still heading in the right direction. Keep abreast of changing market conditions and trends. Monitor customer behavior to stay up-to-date with changing needs. Try to adapt ideas to reach more customers. Groupon started as an online activism platform before changing to end up as the biggest coupon promotion site in the world.[245]

---

242. http://techcrunch.com/2010/07/25/fawlty-logic/
243. http://en.wikipedia.org/wiki/Technology_adoption_lifecycle
244. http://blog.mixpanel.com/2012/11/15/aarrr-mixpanel-for-pirates/
245. http://www.fastcompany.com/1844311/groupon-and-its-pivots-mega-meta-mash-news

Support It After It Goes Live

Support projects until they can support themselves.

"Success is not final, failure is not fatal: it is the courage to continue that counts."
—Winston Churchill, prime minister of the United Kingdom, 1940–1945 and 1951–1955

The Problem

Companies walk away and start new projects without allocating the resources needed to support ideas after they go live.

The Solution

Support projects once they are out in the real world so they can realize their full potential.

- Create a support plan. Factor in costs for ongoing maintenance. List resources and tasks required for routine support and improvements based on usability testing and monitoring of data analytics.

- See it as the start of a race. Now that a project is live, set your sights on the next phase of the project. Agile development and the lean-startup methodology focus on delivering a minimum viable product,[246] giving you money and time left over to spend on iterative improvements. Use this time and money wisely.

- Monitor performance. Keep track of progress using click-track analysis and other data-analysis methods. Follow best practices to set up a dashboard,[247] giving up-to-date statistics of key metrics. Attend to any underperforming areas.

---

246. http://econsultancy.com/uk/blog/10441-the-what-and-how-of-minimum-viable-products
247. http://www.slideshare.net/markginnebaugh/business-intelligence-dashboard-design-best-practices

Ingredient 96

Risk Getting Fired

You see most clearly when you've got nothing to lose.

"If you aren't fired with enthusiasm, you will be fired with enthusiasm."
— Vince Lombardi, American football coach

The Problem

Teams who fear making mistakes will never try anything different to change the world.

The Solution

Stand up for something you believe in, and back it up by taking risks that show your conviction. Become an innovation subversive.[248]

- Prove it works first. Set up a crack team to create a proof of concept that demonstrates your way is a better way. This puts you in a far more powerful position than before, when your ideas were just opinions. If you decide to quit, at least you will have left on a high note.

- Change the scenery. See if you can move into a more interesting role,[249] even if it doesn't exist yet. Come up with a business proposition that covers all the benefits, and pitch it to your boss and potential new boss. Get a mentor to advise you. If it will make you happier and the business gains something valuable, it should be a win-win situation.

- Start your own company. If you're ready, quit and let those who can support your new venture know what you plan to do so you can hit the ground running. Understand the consequences of your decision, though, so you don't go into it blindly.[250] With the right expectations, preparation, expertise, and clients, there's no reason you can't be successful.

248. http://www.innovationinpractice.com/innovation_in_practice/2008/01/innovation-subv.html
249. http://www.thoughtleadersllc.com/2011/02/3-steps-to-successfully-move-into-new/
250. http://www.forbes.com/sites/womensmedia/2013/01/03/should-you-find-a-job-or-start-a-business/

Ingredient 97

Make One Last Attempt

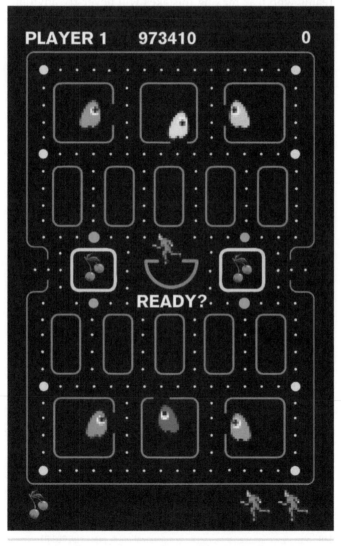

Learn from your mistakes and have one last go.

"First they ignore you, then they laugh at you, then they fight you, then you win."
—Mahatma Gandhi, the preeminent leader of Indian nationalism in British-ruled India

The Problem

Businesses give up too early and stop teams from delivering what's possible because they don't know how to learn from failure to keep going.

The Solution

Learn from mistakes, assess the damage, and see if it makes sense to have one last go.

- Admit mistakes. Learn from the past to move on. Make a public apology and clearly outline how you will address any wrongdoings to regain the trust of your customers and stakeholders. Brands can't be perfect all the time, so hearing a leader admit a mistake and want to make amends makes people feel more at ease and believe things will improve in time.[251] Be human by showing genuine empathy, generosity, and humility to get a second chance.

- Get back to basics. Remember what you are good at and stop pretending to be anything else. Focus on what you can deliver well. See if you can improve the quality of experiences with a smaller set of quality features. Be the best you can at fewer things. Remember, Google's search engine is just a search box,[252] albeit a very powerful, forgiving, and useful one.

- Help them change. Show customers how easy it is to switch over from a competitor. Sky TV does this by clearly highlighting the benefits compared to competitors and having a dedicated Switching Squad that talks to existing providers for you.[253]

---

251. http://www.forbes.com/sites/peterhimler/2012/09/28/leaders-apologize/
252. http://www.businessweek.com/stories/2005-10-02/online-extra-googles-search-for-simplicity
253. http://www.sky.com/shop/switching-to-sky/broadband/

Get Them Addicted

Keep them coming back for more.

"Make a habit of two things: to help; or at least to do no harm."
—Hippocrates, physician and one of the most outstanding
figures in the history of medicine

The Problem

Teams don't put in extra effort to make their products really
special, so customers look elsewhere for their fix.

The Solution

Give customers something they can't get enough of. Make
them long for your product experience.

- Make it enjoyable. Give customers a good reason to use
  your product instead of a competitor's. Provide a useful
  tool, make it supereasy to use, help them learn an
  important skill, and reward them for their time. Kiip,
  for example, is a mobile app that rewards users with
  relevant vouchers for achieving new levels in a game
  they are playing.[254]

- Provide sustenance. Help customers reach and hold on
  to a desired emotion. Design experiences that satisfy
  them and keep them coming back for more when they
  need it. For instance, Flipboard aggregates up-to-date
  technology, lifestyle, and design news from the most
  popular websites, saving users the time and effort of
  finding that news from the individual sources.[255]

- Give them more. Let customers discover new and
  interesting content each time they come back. Spotify is
  a good example; the music service lets users enjoy music
  their friends are listening to at that moment in time, as
  well as build personal playlists and get related artist
  recommendations for free each time they come back.[256]

---

254. http://www.kiip.me/
255. http://flipboard.com/
256. http://www.spotify.com/

Take the Blame

Be more human and forgive to be forgiven.

"It was pride that changed angels into devils; it is humility that makes men as angels."
—Saint Augustine, doctor of the Roman Catholic Church

The Problem

Companies who pretend to have no flaws or weaknesses put up walls to stop customers from getting too close. But when they fail, customers don't hesitate to leave.

The Solution

- Admit mistakes.[257] It's far better to come clean than to have people hear about it from another source. Outline what happened, show you will make amends, and put measures in place to stop it from happening again. Use popular social-media sites like Facebook and Twitter, as well as industry blogs, to formally apologize. Don't be shy.

- Be transparent.[258] Once you have admitted a mistake, follow up a promise to make improvements with an easy way to notify customers of progress. Allows users to sign up and receive alerts, discuss topics of interest on forums, and even go as far as rewarding customers for their patience with a gesture of goodwill—for example, a discount on their current service.

- Work with customers to get it right. Incorporate human evaluation to improve your service offering.[259] Don't second-guess what they want, but instead find ways to incorporate implicit and explicit feedback to better define, teach, and tailor experiences around specific personal preferences. This form of crowdsourcing will make your services more human, social, and useful.

---

257. http://www.trendwatching.com/trends/flawsome/
258. http://techcrunch.com/2012/12/06/apple-ceo-tim-cook-talks-transparency-100m-u-s-mac-manufacturing-investment-forstall-maps-and-more/
259. http://en.wikipedia.org/wiki/Interactive_evolutionary_computation

Give It Away

Give more to get more.

"To do good is noble. To tell others to do good is even nobler and much less trouble."
—Mark Twain, author and humorist

The Problem

Teams don't share their experience or knowledge, making it difficult to reuse the good work done elsewhere internally.

The Solution

Foster an environment of trust and creativity, where ideas can flow and be shared among teams and departments.

- Share knowledge. Show other team members what you have learned, and they will reciprocate. Help others learn new skills, discuss insights, and apply lessons learned. Foster a willingness to help, try ideas, and be less averse to new, risky opportunities. Make your needs known so others understand how best to help when you need it most.

- Make it free.[260] Decide who and what you can give time to for free. This attitude of selfless giving allows teams to donate their expertise freely without any hidden agendas, helping not-for-profit organizations and charities and knowing it is for a good cause.

- Open-source it. The beauty of code that has unlimited expert support means you can develop experiences and connect to other devices to create truly ubiquitous ecosystems, where everyone has a shared interest in making it work. There really is no limit.[261]

---

260. http://www.forbes.com/sites/ashoka/2013/01/21/a-step-by-step-guide-to-giving-half-of-your-work-away-for-free/

261. http://www.forbes.com/sites/parmyolson/2013/01/03/among-the-hot-trends-for-ces-2013-cars-that-run-on-android/

Don't Think You Can Prevent Disaster

Get ready for a surprise.

"Know your enemy and know yourself and you can fight a hundred battles without disaster."
—Sun Tzu, military general, strategist, and philosopher

The Problem

Companies spend time preparing for disaster but don't deal with it well when it arrives.

The Solution

Have a plan of action, but more importantly, be ready to react and solve the right problems in the appropriate manner.

- Have a backup plan. Build in safety features and spend money according to the level of disaster likely to occur. Identify and monitor the weakest links. Thinking you can prevent the biggest threats is often referred to as a black-swan event.[262] You can't prevent all disasters, because you won't know what some of them are, usually because they have never happened before. The newer the concept, the larger the factors of safety you need.[263]

- Be ready for action. There's a misconception that the more prepared you are, the safer you will be. The best you can do is to allocate resources to correctly identify and solve problems quickly. Start with a small team, but scale up quickly if required.

- Ask for forgiveness.[264] When things go wrong, be humble and apologize as soon as possible. Say you're sorry publicly if the mistake affected many of your customers. It's better for people to hear about what went wrong from you than from competitors or other customers.

---

262. http://en.wikipedia.org/wiki/Black_swan_theory
263. http://en.wikipedia.org/wiki/Factor_of_safety
264. http://www.trendwatching.com/trends/flawsome/

Part V

Recipes for Success

In this part, I chose ingredients from this book and combined them into recipes that I feel best demonstrate how leading companies used similar ingredients to become successful. The recipes are not comprehensive, and because they are taken from information that is publicly available, in some cases they may not accurately depict what happened behind the scenes if that information isn't part of the public record. The examples are purely representative and I have not worked at any of the companies unless otherwise stated.

A Recipe for Effective Leadership

Inspire people so they follow your example.

Jeff Bezos, CEO of Amazon, is the epitome of what a forward-thinking leader should be. He is the corporate chief others most want to meet and emulate.[265]

Ingredients

 Know What You Control

 Find the Gaps

 Build an A-Team

 Lead by Example

 *Connect the Dots*

 Make It an Adventure

Try these ingredients to help you become a more effective and natural leader.

1. *Know What You Control*

Prepare to uncover problems. Bezos separated personal points of view from business ones, allowing him to react

---

265. http://www.forbes.com/sites/georgeanders/2012/04/04/inside-amazon/

quickly to important changes in the market based on what customers really wanted and what was best for Amazon as a business. Avoid building a "private empire" and underestimating the role of chance, leaving your company at the mercy of uncontrollable circumstances. Factor in surprising insights and react to unforeseen circumstances early to become more successful in the long run.

2. Find the Gaps

Identify what you don't know. Leaders who think they have all the answers don't look for further validation, so end up leading their teams down the wrong path. Dynamic leaders, like Bezos, can confidently make crucial business decisions and deal with crises because they are open enough to trust the knowledge of others to keep them informed. Don't make decisions until you have all the critical facts in hand and have answered important questions and validated key assumptions.

3. Build an A-Team

Hire people you trust can deliver awesome solutions. Work with people who strive to make a real difference and are willing to prove their worth every second of the day. Amazon employees are known as "customer experience bar raisers" and are passionate about tracking and making appropriate recommendations based on customer trends and behavior analysis.[266] This has led to innovative new projects such as the Kindle tablet and ebook readers.

4. Lead by Example

Actions speak louder than words. Bezos once said, "There are two types of companies: those that work hard to charge customers more, and those that work hard to charge customers less. Both approaches can work. We are firmly in the second camp."[267] Many retailers talk about championing customers and passing savings on to them, but few succeed

---

266. http://survey.cvent.com/blog/cvent-web-surveys-blog/customer-focused-10-leadership-lessons-from-jeff-bezos
267. http://thenextweb.com/mobile/2011/09/28/amazons-bezos-we-worked-hard-to-charge-you-less-for-kindle-fire/

as well as Amazon, where "frugality" is one of the official company values.[268]

5. Connect the Dots

Bring parts of your company, teams, and resources together to create more-effective solutions faster. Complaints can be devastating in the age of viral tweets and blog posts. Bezos and his Amazon managers across all disciplines and departments attend two days of call-center training each year. They do this to gain humility and empathy for the customer, which also results in a far better working relationship between departments.[269]

6. Make It an Adventure

Back in 1997 Bezos passionately expressed his excitement for the future: "This is Day 1 for the Internet. We still have so much to learn."[270] At Amazon's new headquarters, two of the largest buildings are Day 1 North and Day 1 South. In interviews Bezos still refers to the Internet as an uncharted world, imperfectly understood and yielding new surprises all the time. This vision has proved hugely attractive to new and existing employees who yearn to be part of the journey of discovery and excitement that is now associated with Amazon.

Tips on How to Apply This Recipe

Don't take on too much at once, or you'll be in danger of starting too many initiatives and not completing any quickly enough. Focus on a few key quick wins to show you are serious and are capable of introducing change that is not only effective, but supported by other parts of the business. Key to becoming an effective leader is to know which rules to break and what new rules to put in place to make a real impact.

Clarify your role and your team's role, and look to improve what is within your control before deciding to grow your circle of influence. Be careful not to step on anyone else's

---

268. http://tinyurl.com/7sqzn2c
269. http://www.forbes.com/sites/georgeanders/2012/04/04/bezos-tips/
270. http://www.forbes.com/sites/georgeanders/2012/04/04/bezos-tips/

toes, but instead leverage the skills within other departments to help you achieve success. Once you have gained the trust of the business, see if it makes sense to incorporate additional resources from other departments as part of your team. For example, bringing visual-design resources into a customer-experience team to improve workflow and ultimately produce a better product design makes good business sense.

Aspire to be a leader who is charismatic, takes the necessary risks, and has a sixth sense for knowing what needs to be done. This is the mentality you and your team need to adopt and promote within your organization to provide relevant disruptive change and instill enough confidence to start making a real difference.

A Recipe for Awesome Employees

Hire the best you can, then nurture them until they can fly.

ThoughtWorks prides itself on hiring and retaining the best. During the time I spent there, I worked with some of the most clever people I've ever met. ThoughtWorks provides a highly creative and engaging environment, as well as the right level of support to keep their employees happy and doing a great job.

Ingredients

 Increase Happiness

 Make It Personal

 Train Them Right

 Make It an Adventure

 Perform as a Team

 *Celebrate Success*

Want to attract and keep the best of the best? Here's how to provide the right environment and opportunities:

1. *Increase Happiness*

Make people proud to be associated with you. Be very clear about what employees are getting themselves into, and make sure the entire project team is aware too. If there are any changes in roles, notify others on the team so there are no surprises. ThoughtWorks hires and retains extremely capable and talented people—being named "Among Best Companies to Work For in 2011-2012" proves the point.[271]

2. *Make It Personal*

Understand what drives people, and help them improve. ThoughtWorks runs targeted psychometric employee evaluations to help identify areas for improvement and opportunities for exploration. A discussion to review the results is held at the employee's earliest availability and in a location of the employee's choice. Relevant concerns and successes are run through before an agreed-upon course of action is put in place to monitor improvements, helping employees continue being as effective and happy as possible. Employees are also given the opportunity to work on one of the many social-impact projects at ThoughtWorks—they can chose the ones that best match their values.

3. *Train Them Right*

Set realistic expectations through practice. Expose new employees to a real work environment as soon as possible. ThoughtWorks runs "ThoughtWorks University," a three-to-six-week immersion program where seasoned Thought-Workers mentor and guide new employees from the start to the end of a project. Working as a real cross-functional team, everyone has to learn to solve problems together to deliver a finished product. Importantly, ThoughtWorks University also provides new joiners with the opportunity to be immersed in the ThoughtWorks culture and values from the get-go.

---

271. http://www.reuters.com/article/2012/01/31/idUS250698+31-Jan-2012+PRN20120131

4. Make It an Adventure

Make it interesting so they will never want to leave. Identify projects that challenge, provide opportunities for growth, and encourage creative experimentation. When they aren't on client projects, ThoughtWorks employees are encouraged to pursue projects or ideas to grow their own knowledge and skills, like trying new technology and approaches. ThoughtWorks also holds monthly evening sessions called Last Thursday, where they make announcements and updates. There are many other events, too (Geek Nights, Code Dojos, Awareness Nights), which means there's something going on every week.

5. Perform as a Team

Let employees know that the team and the wider company is there to support them and help them be the best that they can be. Collaboration, communication, creativity, and flexibility are all traits ThoughtWorkers are encouraged to embrace. Foster an environment of trust, openness, and creativity and embrace change as an opportunity to do even better work. Appreciate and support each other as a team so you can achieve goals more efficiently. Be honest with each other and don't wait until it's too late to let others know if you need help.

6. Celebrate Success

Recognize the hard work people put in. At ThoughtWorks, great individual and team work is internally recognized at monthly get-togethers, individual appraisals, and team feedback sessions. The company takes the time to personally recognize folks who've made outstanding contributions during the year. No good deed goes unnoticed. Great companies realize that happy and capable employees make a company successful, so they do a lot to make sure appreciation doesn't go unexpressed.

Tips on How to Apply This Recipe

Hire people for what they're good at, not what you want them to be good at. People perform best when they are doing what they enjoy most, so it is superimportant that you understand what really drives employees so you can position them within your team to be as effective as possible. Don't wait to recognize and utilize available talent, or you will lose valuable people because they feel unmotivated and underappreciated.

Work with your organization to highlight the biggest "rocks" that need to be moved. Grow your team's capabilities to be effective at delivering what's needed to support your organization's biggest requirements. I work hard to incorporate agile processes, a lean user experience, and lean-startup principles to validate ideas early so that I can quickly make visible what is most valuable with a minimum of investment. I train and hire people who believe in and want to embrace my approach and vision, so there is no doubt in my mind that I have the support of a team with the right mindset for success.

Make the workplace a fun and vibrant place to be to foster a sense of creativity. Give your team the opportunity and environment to grow and experiment while delivering what's needed to improve existing experiences. Customer experience is a hands-on practice that should encourage customers to "play" with ideas to get real and useful feedback.

Inspired by Apple stores, I've created play areas where anyone within the organization, every time they pass our team's open-plan workspace, can pick up a smartphone or a tablet or interact with a desktop or laptop computer with the latest prototypes on them. This reinforces our sense of play and our live customer-validation process, allowing us to run ad hoc usability tests, raise the team profile, and increase team morale. Seeing other parts of the business better understand and appreciate the value we offer, first-hand, is invaluable.

A Recipe for Social Relevance

Get people talking, sharing, and promoting who you are.

Foursquare seems to always come third, after Facebook and Twitter, when we think about social networks. However, it has strengths—for example, location-based, real-time rewards—that both of the other social-networking giants don't, as well as many of the ones they do.

Ingredients

 *Understand Customer Needs*

 Promote Your Team

 Crowdsource It

 Find the Sweet Spot

 Make It Personal

 Reward Them

Connecting with consumers directly to build an active online community is the holy grail of any company that wants to promote its brand through the power of social networking. Try combining these ingredients to create a loyal community that hangs out with you forever.

1. Understand Customer Needs

Embrace customer beliefs and work toward their goals. Foursquare users "check in" so they can be recognized as the first to discover a place and note what's good and bad about it. Identifying brand advocates who thrive on recommending your products and services to their peers is one of the best ways of building trust in your offering. Make these advocates happy, and they will help you attract more customers.

2. Promote Your Team

Give customers insight into your cause and beliefs; tell them how it all started, include the war stories, and help them identify with people involved in your organization. Show them how your solution fits their lifestyle, and be completely transparent about your intentions. Get customers to connect and empathize with your brand to start building a superloyal relationship.

3. Crowdsource It

Make participants feel like part of a community that can effect change, and make sure this change is apparent. Empower close-knit communities that support each other by allowing them to share what they think, do, and feel. Foursquare has created interactions that allow peer-to-peer content creation, sharing, and sourcing of appropriate solutions.

4. Find the Sweet Spot

Not every social interaction is done with one brand or through one channel alone. Understand where your customers socialize online and offline to deliver an enhanced experience by connecting these disparate aspects together. Foursquare is a location-based online community that relies on users exploring and checking in online when experiencing real-world places. By joining the online digital world with the offline real one, Foursquare has created an environment where real people can enjoy their real-world experiences with others in the digital world.

5. Make It Personal

Give users profiles they can fine-tune to filter out unwanted content and experiences and keep useful ones in. Like someone you know, Foursquare can recommend things you may like and remind you of past experiences based on your interactions, both positive and negative. Become a useful friend who knows who customers are, and be able to help them find what they want and avoid things they will not like.

6. Reward Them

Reward people for using your service and sharing their experiences. Foursquare does this with offers and specials that include vouchers users can redeem at real stores. Users can also earn and unlock badges based on the frequency and type of check-in. The more unique badges a user unlocks, the more respect he receives. Foursquare also makes it supereasy to share and notify others of these rewards on customers' other social networks.

Tips on How to Apply This Recipe

Try to create a platform and an ecosystem that let customers naturally interact and express themselves around topics they enjoy. Make it easy for them to engage where they want, how they want, and with whom they want at any time. Make people comfortable being who they are with others who share a common interest or belief. I conduct customer behavioral research to fine-tune experiences, making them less intrusive and more relevant and engaging.

Don't underestimate the power people have within their social groups. Be quick to recognize individual expertise, and let customers naturally influence those who identify with their points of view. Peer recommendations are important; adding this extra layer of validation will help customers make more-confident decisions. Customer views are always high on my list when creating any experience where a sense of community is important.

Gamify the experience by giving customers extra incentive to continue using your product or service. Try thanking customers for their loyalty with real-world rewards so they can claim food or drink in their favorite hangouts, for example. Sometimes a reflection of peer validation—for example, as a number of sales, follows, shares, comments, or emails, as well as seeing their name high up on a leaderboard—is enough. This form of social validation is also very important—just knowing your points of view are valuable to others feels great.

A Recipe for Lean Startup in Large Organizations

Do the minimum and fine-tune what you've got.

Lean startups validate their business models by testing their products or services with real customers early and often. There's absolutely no reason why large organizations can't embrace this philosophy to get cross-platform digital experiences validated within weeks of discussing an idea. I set up HaaYaa,[272] a cooperative of highly creative and skilled individuals, to help large organizations create and refine proof-of-concept prototypes until there are no doubts that customers really want these organizations' new products and services. At the same time, I ensure these organizations meet important business requirements. Being big doesn't mean you can't think small.

Ingredients

Test Your Biggest Hypothesis First

Slice It Thinly

Timebox It

Fail Fast, Fail Often

Check the Data

---

272. http://HaaYaa.com

 *Build Up Enough Momentum*

Looking to create awesome experiences that customers actually want and that businesses will see as a good investment? These ingredients will keep you lean, mean, and superkeen:

1. Test Your Biggest Hypothesis First

Test risky and mission-critical assumptions as early as possible. If you don't prove or disprove these first, you will waste time building on unproven facts. I have taken unproven assumptions about what customers like or dislike, and used them to create digital concepts that can be tested within the first few weeks of the start of most projects—first in focus groups and later as interactive HTML prototypes. These can include new navigation ideas, payment models, and innovative interactions on mobile devices, tablets, and interactive TV.

2. Slice It Thinly

Do the minimum needed to test your idea effectively. Focus on key functionality to get your core value proposition across clearly. Ensure the correct brand messaging is in place and aim to delight customers. I encourage putting systems into place for frequent and early testing of digital prototypes. This allows basic value-added services like saving or sharing to be validated before advanced features, such as personalization, are added. Build in more depth of functionality after you're confident that the basics are in place and that you have created a core set of services customers find really useful.

3. Timebox It

Limiting the time to achieve tasks and still delivering something of value takes discipline, creative thinking, and a whole lot of trust. Start by prioritizing what's important, and allow time to make changes when you fine-tune ideas later. I empower customer-experience teams to work with the entire business to reduce the time needed to complete tasks while still raising the dev and user-experience quality bar. Shortening the time to complete and validate ideas means there is time to fine-tune and enhance ideas once they had been through usability testing. Be clear about what needs to be achieved in the time given, though.

4. Fail Fast, Fail Often

Get stakeholders to acknowledge it's best to know as early as possible what does not work. Treat each stage of a project as an experiment you can learn from to make improvements. I urge customer-experience teams to run successive rapid iterative tests and evaluations to get customer validation and reveal new insight.[273] I also challenge design and development teams to make improvements quickly between subsequent tests.

5. Check the Data

Identify data across key experiences that indicate success and failure. Analyze the data; gain enough insight and validated learning to make improvements. To keep track of the results of these improvements, I set up customer-experience teams to work with data-analytics teams on monitoring usage stats to see each improvement's effect on groups of cohorts.[274] I also recommend running multivariate tests on variations of a design concept to see which one is most successful.[275]

6. Build Up Enough Momentum

Make continuous improvements until you have a product or service that truly delights. Multiple projects owned by different parts of the organization are usually run in parallel. The core functionality, enhancements, and new features of each project are tested, and then they are quickly connected, retested, and refined into one holistic experience. Constantly challenge, test for usability, and keep fine-tuning from proof

---

273. http://www.questionablemethods.com/2012/09/rite-testing-brings-team-together.html
274. http://cutroni.com/blog/2012/12/11/cohort-analysis-with-google-analytics/
275. https://www.optimizely.com/resources/multivariate-test-vs-ab-test

of concept throughout delivery, until the customer experience hangs together well enough to go live.

Tips on How to Apply This Recipe

Start with small projects and show success quickly. Once these have proven to work, tackle larger projects. Find other departments you can approach, and show them the benefits of being involved in a new and more successful way of doing things.

Try to get buy-in from peer and senior management. (I've been able get CEOs, CTOs, and CIOs to buy into the value of customer-experience design.) For example, you might agree to bring native mobile-operating-system design and front-end development resources into the customer-experience team. This can improve and speed up proof-of-concept creation, validation, and design iteration.

I'm a huge lean-startup and lean-user-experience fan. Having worked for large media companies in the roles of design director and head of customer experience, I have always championed the need for early customer validation. I used the insight gained to reassess business needs and evolve projects to make them more relevant and effective before launch. I've also implemented post-launch support systems, using continuous design and improvement to ensure projects preserve their relevancy.

A Recipe for Being Indispensable

Create something customers can't live without.

Dropbox founder Drew Houston created a personal cloud-storage solution after repeatedly forgetting his USB flash drive while studying at MIT. By 2011, Dropbox held more than fourteen percent of the worldwide backup-client market.[276]

Ingredients

Understand Customer Needs

Be Really Good at One Thing

Keep It Simple

Align with Expectations

Make It Accessible

Get Them Addicted

Here is how you, too, can cook up something people want to use all the time.

---

276. http://en.wikipedia.org/wiki/Dropbox_(service)

1. Understand Customer Needs

Observe what really annoys customers and come up with ideas to remove their frustration. Drew realized existing cloud-storage services had problems with Internet latency, large-file storage, and usability. After creating Dropbox for himself, he realized others could benefit from it too.

2. Be Really Good at One Thing

Be the best at one thing rather than OK at many things. People trust brands with products and services focused on one area so they don't have to think too hard if they have to make a choice. Dropbox is the easiest way to back up, access, and share digital content from any desktop or mobile device.

3. Keep It Simple

Design something simple and reliable that fits with the way people work. Dropbox automatically saves and syncs updated files, and is easily accessible via any operating system's info bar.

4. Align with Expectations

Let users do what they want to do. Give them the freedom to adapt your service to meet specific needs. Power users found ways to enhance Dropbox functionality, like file-sending via Gmail, remote application launching, and system monitoring. Dropbox continuously optimizes its service, encouraging innovative user-driven ideas such as these to increase usage.

5. Make It Accessible

Get it to work seamlessly on any device. In response to the launch of Google Drive and Microsoft's SkyDrive, Dropbox allowed users to automatically upload content from cameras, tablets, SD cards, and smartphones at no extra cost. Dropbox also provides client software for Microsoft Windows, Apple Mac OS, Linux, Google Android, Apple iOS, BlackBerry OS, and all popular web browsers.

6. Get Them Addicted

Employ gamification techniques to motivate people to continue using your services.[277] Show them how to stay active and remain influential within their peer groups, socially competing to be one up all the time. Don't forget to reward them for their efforts. Dropbox lets users gain more storage space simply by getting people they know to sign up.

Tips on How to Apply This Recipe

Simplicity and a great customer experience play a big part in creating a product or service that customers will want to integrate into their lives. Start by reducing the number of features, and improving this core set until the features become the best they can be.

Define what success looks like. Realistically evaluate business success metrics by building proofs of concept and validating them with customers to see if they can be achieved. Reset expectations and look for other ways to create business success, factoring in customer behaviors, trends, and needs.

Test, test, test. Validate your ideas with customers and be ready to keep evolving them until your customer and business success metrics show you have a useful experience. Work with parts of the business to gain required insight if needed to provide your business or client with alternative and additional opportunities, backed up with research and usability-test feedback.

---

277. http://www.forbes.com/sites/realspin/2013/02/21/can-gamificatio-save-our-broken-education-system/

A Recipe for Evolution

Disruptive technologies have increased TV's reach and engagement.

Samsung has gradually become the most innovative HDTV brand. Early in 2013 the company announced that all its next-generation TVs would allow customers to use voice or gesture control to get to content.[278]

Ingredients

 Make It Easy

 Increase Happiness

 Improve vs. Differentiate

 Time It Right

 *Don't Do It All*

 Know What Competitors Are Up To

---

278. http://www.forbes.com/sites/ericsavitz/2013/01/07/ces-samsung-unveils-4k-tvs-upgrades-smart-tv-service/

Whether you are new to the game or a wise old sage, this recipe will help evolve your ideas so they always remain relevant.

1. Make It Easy

Make it easy for your existing customers to experience the latest technology. At the Consumer Electronics Show in January 2013, Samsung announced that its Evolution Kit would allow existing Smart TV customers to enjoy the latest interactive services without having to purchase a new TV.[279]

2. Increase Happiness

Keep delighting customers by understanding what matters most to them and improving their experience to match their expectations. Samsung realizes that innovation means new interaction models that customers will need to familiarize themselves with, so the company invested many hours creating a delightful onboarding journey to make the learning and content-discovery experience an amazing and memorable one.[280]

3. Improve vs. Differentiate

Be better than everyone else. Samsung the world's largest commercial ultrahigh-definition TV built, the award-winning S9000. The TV uses new LED technology to deliver the brightest pictures ever, and it set a new industry standard for picture quality.[281]

4. Time It Right

Samsung Ventures invested $5 million in TV ecommerce platform Delivery Agent.[282] Delivery Agent's development of apps for TVs and tablets fits well with Samsung's current and future smartphone, tablet, and television product plans.

---

279. http://global.samsungtomorrow.com/?p=21039
280. http://www.engadget.com/2012/12/25/samsung-UI-refresh/
281. http://global.samsungtomorrow.com/?p=21335
282. http://www.deliveryagent.com/2012/12/delivery-agent-secures-5-million-investment-from-samsung-venture-investment-corporation/

5. Don't Do It All

Partner up with someone who will make you more awesome. Leverage each other's strengths to fill in gaps that would have been difficult for you to fill on your own. In November 2012, Yahoo! and Samsung formed a multiyear partnership to deliver interactive TV,[283] allowing Samsung Smart TV owners to receive real-time, actionable content alongside TV shows and commercials.

6. Know What Competitors Are Up To

Don't let anyone beat you to it. If you believe competitors are not playing ball, do what's needed to set things right. Samsung filed an injunction against LG, accusing it of engineering leaks.[284]

Tips on How to Apply This Recipe

Make adoption of future experiences as easy and painless as possible. You may have a world-changing idea, but if it is hard to understand and customers aren't motivated enough to want to adopt it, it will fail. Start by trying something new based on what has already been successful, and make it better in at least one way.

Public relations is very important, and it can be anything from low-cost viral marketing, where customer advocates help spread the word about what you are doing, to having a stand at important industry events to promote your new product or service. Whatever your budget or method, make sure it's timely and appropriate—but most importantly, make sure it's done.

Partnering up, purchasing a third-party capability, or being acquired yourself are all options to help you evolve. If the focus is to enable a good idea to become more readily available to a larger target audience in a shorter time frame, then you really need to consider these seriously. After all, a successful evolution means staying alive.

---

283. http://www.businesswire.com/news/home/20121105006517/en/Yahoo!-Samsung-Form-Multi-year-Partnership-Deliver-Interactive

284. http://english.yonhapnews.co.kr/national/2012/09/05/27/0302000000AEN20120905007900315F.HTML

A Recipe for Constant Innovation

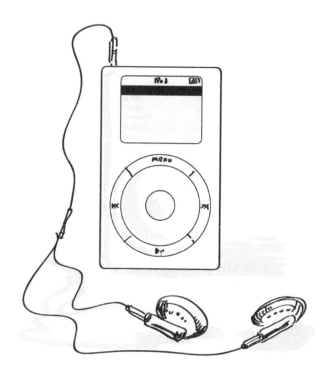

Innovative products define history.

Apple is one of the most valuable companies in the world, with a market cap larger than that of Google and Microsoft combined.[285]

Ingredients

 Build an A-Team

 *Test Your Biggest Hypothesis First*

 *Challenge and Disrupt*

 Create a Tipping Point

 *Keep It Under the Radar*

 Stay Hungry, Stay Foolish

---

285. http://www.dailymail.co.uk/sciencetech/article-2099511/Apple-worth-Microsoft-Google-combined.html

Here is how you, too, can continuously cook up exciting products that new and existing users just can't get enough of.

1. Build an A-Team

One team can transform an entire organization.[286] Find that unique set of awesome, capable, self-motivated individuals and push them to achieve the impossible. This should not be an exclusive club, and you can have more than one of these teams, but they do need to be separated from the rest of the business so as not to get distracted from creating that game-changing idea. This is what Apple did when designing the iPod.

2. Test Your Biggest Hypothesis First

If you're going to change the world, you'd better have some big assumptions to test. To break into the MP3 market, Apple had to create a totally different way of consuming digital music.[287] The biggest assumption was that consumers could access an online music library (the iTunes Store) using their iPods and store music for playback later. That assumption proved true, giving Apple a powerful new product and service with which to enter the consumer-electronics world.

3. Challenge and Disrupt

Spot a really bad way of doing things, then improve it. The iTunes Store was set up to support the launch of the iPod and became the easiest way to purchase digital music, video, and audiobooks. Major record labels gave up their own content-download experiments when the iTunes Store became the standard for digital content discovery and purchasing. Every song was the same price—ninety-nine cents —and users could purchase songs individually or by the album with the click of a button. Simple.

4. Create a Tipping Point

Fine-tune your service offering until it fits naturally in customers' lives. Apple realized that consumers were looking for products they could identify with that would be an

---

286. http://www.fastcompany.com/1692625/how-team-apple-made-ipod-dream-reality
287. http://www.theglobeandmail.com/technology/digital-culture/how-the-ipod-changed-everything/article556167/?page=all

extension of their personality. The iPod advertising campaign showed how fun and customizable iPods were, featuring chart-topping hits like U2's "Vertigo" and Coldplay's "Viva la Vida."[288] Consumers instantly saw how the product fit with their lifestyles, and sales shot through the roof. Consumers found it cool to be associated with a product and a brand that allowed them to express themselves.

5. Keep It Under the Radar

Do it differently, do it well, and do it so they go, "Wow!" When Steve Jobs introduced the iPod in 2001,[289] you could hear the audience gasp in amazement. The design had been kept under wraps until the very last moment. Competitors had to completely rethink sales, marketing, and product strategies. Surprise and anticipation are now signature Apple approaches when unveiling a product or service. Give target audiences what they crave and satisfy their deepest desires.

6. Stay Hungry, Stay Foolish

Stay inquisitive and never tire of challenging the status quo. Keep disrupting and asking "Why not?" If someone says you can't but you believe you can, do it. The iPod established Apple as a serious consumer-product company. Steve Jobs and Apple found a winning formula, creating innovative products like the iPhone to prove critics wrong about the need for such devices. As a result Apple became one of the largest mobile phone–makers, joining Samsung and Nokia.[290] Who says you can't dream big and do it?

Tips on How to Apply This Recipe

Keep innovation projects and teams separate from tactical and optimization (bug fixes and so on) ones. Don't make the mistake of thinking the same people can innovate, work on tactical projects, and fix current live feature experiences. I find that there's always a compromise on the level of innovation because people get too busy with tactical work. I prefer having separate teams all producing results.

---

288. http://www.admadness.co/2010/11/ipod-advertising-campaign/
289. http://www.youtube.com/watch?v=kN0SVBCJqLs
290. http://blogs.strategyanalytics.com/WDS/post/2013/02/01/Apple-Becomes-Largest-Mobile-Phone-Vendor-in-United-States-in-Q4-2012.aspx

Focus on innovative ideas that solve the biggest customer problems. See if these ideas fit with your organization's future vision, but be prepared to adapt that vision if you can prove there is an opportunity to really own and disrupt a new area. *The Sun* newspaper tries to cram in as much content as possible and push that to its readers. To attract new customers and introduce a new paid-for subscription model, I focus on pushing easier-to-use yet far more-personalized experiences through digital devices like smartphones and tablets. Considering the device and use cases for consumption means delivering a shorter but more-relevant experience.

Don't share too much too soon with too many people. Create your innovative idea in its undiluted form and test it with target customers. Use real feedback and results to persuade stakeholders to invest the extra time and effort to make it a reality. It's the only way.

A Recipe for Getting Investment

Put on a good show.

Only a small percentage of ideas get funded. We can pivot, evolve, and present a perfect pitch, but what does it really take to get investment? Instagram built a fun photo-sharing and social-networking tool, attracted a huge number of users, and made strategic moves that culminated in Facebook buying the company for $1 billion in April 2012.[291]

Ingredients

 Start with the End

 Build an A-Team

 Align with Expectations

 Be Really Good at One Thing

 *Build Up Enough Momentum*

 Time It Right

Here is how you, too, can cook up something extremely attractive and have investors clambering over each other to get a piece of you.

1. Start with the End

Give people a clear picture of what they need to do. Lay out a clear road map of features and make sure team members are aware of their roles and share the same vision. Founders

---

291. http://www.bbc.co.uk/news/technology-17658264

Kevin Systrom and Michel Krieger started Burbn before it became Instagram.[292] They knew what they wanted and took clear first steps toward achieving it by focusing on mobile photography and a simple check-in process.

2. Build an A-Team

Investors love teams that show potential beyond the idea they are buying. Pull together a group of people who can work well together and keep coming up with great ideas. Start small, keep the team lean, and show why each person is vital to success. Instagram had only thirteen employees when Facebook invested.[293] Investors buy into people first, then the product or service.

3. Align with Expectations

Fill a gap in an investor's portfolio. Show you can improve a key performance indicator more quickly than the investor can. Research what investors are looking for and evolve your ideas where appropriate to fit with their current and future business strategies. Although Facebook had its own photo-upload feature, Facebook still bought Instagram just before going public. Stay ahead of the investor curve in a given market to prove there is potential in your idea.

4. Be Really Good at One Thing

Don't throw too much into the mix; focus on one key competitive differentiator and make it as unique as possible. Investors see many companies, so make sure they remember the one thing you are good at. Instagram created simple digital photo filters that allowed hundreds of millions of users to express their individuality; nothing else came close in terms of ease of use.

5. Build Up Enough Momentum

Show a steady stream of loyal customers using your service. Show that this is on the incline and that with each new release or new idea you attract new customers as well as

---

292. http://gigaom.com/2010/03/05/burbn-funded-for-html-5-version-of-foursquare/
293. http://www.dailymail.co.uk/news/article-2127343/Facebook-buys-Instagram-13-employees-share-100m-CEO-Kevin-Systrom-set-make-400m.html

please existing customers who just can't get enough of your brand. Instagram had 1 million users in December 2010, 12 million in October 2011, and more than 14 million by December 2011. In July 2012, the company announced it had more than 80 million accounts set up.[294]

6. Time It Right

Understand the consequences of strategic plays. Don't jump the gun. Time it right, and the rewards will be huge. The day the Android version of Instagram was released, it was downloaded more than 1 million times. That same week it received $50 million from venture capitalists for a share of the company.[295] A few days later, Facebook acquired Instagram for approximately $1 billion in cash and stock.

Tips on How to Apply This Recipe

It's important to know what success looks like. Track what's really important. If you can't track it, you can't prove it. To show how a concept has achieved success, I work with customer-analytics teams to set up dashboards and reporting tools that alert my team if any metric falls below an acceptable level, helping us decide what we need to do to improve a service offering.

Make it supereasy to understand what you're doing. Show how you meet a customer need by providing a service in a unique way. When pitching your idea, prove there is customer interest and clearly outline how what you are asking for will be spent wisely and frugally. This applies to startups as well as when you're persuading internal stakeholders to invest enough in an idea to back it and produce it.

I find the easiest way to get investment is to show proof of interest, differentiation, and a clear plan of action, which are all necessary to realize even more potential quickly.

---

294. http://news.cnet.com/8301-1023_3-57480931-93/instagram-passes-80-million-users/

295. http://techcrunch.com/2012/04/09/right-before-acquisition-instagram-closed-50m-at-a-500m-valuation-from-sequoia-thrive-greylock-and-benchmark/

A Recipe for Doing Social Good

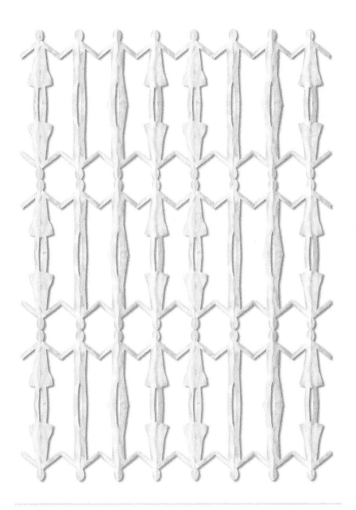

Make the world a better place, just because you can.

RapidFTR (Family Tracing and Reunification)[296] is an open source mobile-phone app that helps locate and reunite lost children during conflict in war-torn third-world countries. It is run by the Child Protection in Emergencies team at UNICEF. I worked on Blackberry mobile-interface designs that allowed field representatives to capture information about lost people quickly and efficiently.

Ingredients

   Promote Your Team

   Make It Personal

   *Don't Jump to Conclusions*

   *Frame It*

---

296. http://www.rapidftr.com

Crowdsource It

 Increase Happiness

Do the right thing, and people will care about you and your company even more. Here's how to get that halo above your head.

1. *Promote Your Team*

Remember, it's never about you and always about someone else's happiness and success. Find a noble cause that fits with your company's beliefs as well as your own, and find a way to support it. RapidFTR fit in well with my hunger to do something meaningful and change the world. I wanted to work on a project where I could personally make a difference to help people in truly dire conditions.

2. *Make It Personal*

Get your team members to identify with the problem. Once they can relate to it, they won't think twice about helping out. Manage expectations by clarifying their role to leverage their strengths, especially if they're giving up free time for the project. Appeal to personal goals for extra motivation. As a child I got lost for a few minutes before my parents found me. Children and family members can be separated for months at a time in Uganda. Relating to the feeling of being lost and knowing what it feels like to be found again made me want to work on the project even more.

3. *Don't Jump to Conclusions*

Factor in technological and cultural differences to deliver the right solution. Find out who it's for, when they'll use it, and what constraints and dependencies there are. In Uganda none of the RapidFTR aid workers locating lost family members had a smartphone. The first design challenge was to create an experience that could work on older Blackberry phones. Until the right mass channel of delivery was considered, it was difficult to know if users would incorporate this type of service into their daily lives.

4. Frame It

Help your team empathize. Try appealing to multiple senses to heighten their view of reality. RapidFTR created a short video to highlight the seriousness of the plight.[297] Draw direct comparisons to family life and what the loss of a loved one can be like, and ask for a sacrifice of a relatively small amount of time and money to help solve these problems. For example, the price of a cup of coffee each day can pay for aid workers to go out in the field to capture information and better conduct their inquiries and searches.

5. Crowdsource It

Many social-good projects rely on volunteers sacrificing their own time and effort. RapidFTR crowdsourced its volunteers from around the world, across different time zones.[298] When I worked on the project I was working with developers in New York, Australia, Africa, India, and the United Kingdom. Where there is a will, there's a way.

6. Increase Happiness

The satisfaction you get from launching a social-good project outweighs any difficulties you may face delivering it. RapidFTR continues to help reunite lost children with their families, reducing the time and confusion normally associated with family-reunification projects. Knowing that you and your team have made a really important, life-changing difference makes it all worthwhile. This level of happiness is known as living a meaningful life.[299]

---

297. http://vimeo.com/28124898
298. http://www.forbes.com/sites/dell/2012/06/07/crowdsourcing-social-good-and-innovation-3/
299. http://www.ted.com/talks/martin_seligman_on_the_state_of_psychology.html

Tips on How to Apply This Recipe

Try infusing social-good values into your organization's mission statement to include social and economic justice, service to others, society over self, and doing the right thing. It might make you feel better about who you are working for and clarify why you are doing it.

Use social good to train yourself to understand constraints and be able to factor in new requirements. In the RapidFTR example, the constraints were the lack of smartphones for which to design an experience, and the lack of a good mobile-network infrastructure, which made it hard to deliver and save up-to-date information.

Adopt a social-good mindset to add a sense of responsibility to everything you do. Customers will appreciate the fact that you stand for making the world a better place and are not putting other agendas, like financial profit or world domination, ahead of what will be good for human beings and the planet. It will also help you make better decisions about how best to portray your organization's products and services and give your company a human face when you put customer needs first. This mindset serves particularly well in customer-service scenarios, where empathy for solving the most urgent problems is superimportant.

A Recipe for World Domination

Take over the world by continuously delivering innovation and value.

Google is just a search engine, right? Actually it is also a mobile OS, a laptop, a pair of glasses, a car, a map...

Ingredients

Improve vs. Differentiate

Simplify Your Business Model

Cast It Far, Then Reel It In

Keep It Simple

Give It Away

Be Childish

Identify with what the world needs, and you can do anything. Here's how to play a part in everyone's lives.

1. Improve vs. Differentiate

Google constantly readapts its products and services based on changing market demands. One of its main focuses is on improving the accuracy and flexibility of the Google search algorithm.[300] Google realizes that having a great idea doesn't mean there isn't a competitor already working on a similar idea. That knowledge keeps Google on its toes to remain a market leader.

2. Simplify Your Business Model

Like all the best ideas, innovation occurs only when you are brave enough to remove, combine, or focus on concepts that will make a real difference. Google responded to a potential economic crisis by reapportioning time spent mainly on its Google Apps for Business subscription model—the sell side—and focusing more efforts on the buy side.[301]

3. Cast It Far, Then Reel It In

Google loves crazy and "impossible" ideas. This gives the company a chance to flex its innovation muscles. Although some of Google's innovations have been successful, many haven't.[302] Google continues to make bets that aren't going to scale successfully, and many that fail. But every time the company makes progress toward changing the world. It is difficult to stick to your beliefs while delivering something people want. But do it—Google does.

4. Keep It Simple

Reduce the time it takes to complete tasks. Make features really intuitive so there is little doubt what they are meant to do.[303] The technology that powers Google's search engine is, of course, anything but simple. But the actual experience of those fancy algorithms is something that would satisfy a Shaker: a clean, white home page, typically featuring no

---

300. http://googleappengine.blogspot.co.uk/2010/02/scalability-means-flexibili-ty.html
301. http://www.telco2.net/blog/2009/04/google_and_the_art_of_twosided.html
302. http://thenextweb.com/google/2012/09/08/is-google-innovative-tech-company-planet/
303. http://en.wikipedia.org/wiki/Affordance

more than thirty lean words; a cheery, six-character, primary-colored logo; and a capacious search box. It couldn't be friendlier or easier to use.[304]

5. Give It Away

The choice of operating systems for cars is of growing importance to manufacturers as consumers become more fickle and knowledgeable. Google's Android OS now runs many car navigation systems.[305] The platform is open source; carmakers can customize what they need.

6. Find Allies

It can be cost-effective to buy a company and integrate it into your own if it makes sense strategically. Google has bought more than 100 companies since 2001, including Android Inc., which allowed it to move into the mobile-operating-system marketplace; YouTube, which allowed it to become the largest social video platform; and DoubleClick to integrate into its AdSense service.

Tips on How to Apply This Recipe

The world is constantly changing. Don't expect to stay at the top of your game or aim to get there if you aren't prepared to adapt and look at new areas of growth. Google started off as a search engine and now has spread its wings to innovate in new and exciting areas no one thought the company would dominate.

Make it easy to decide. I recently worked on designing digital experiences for a large supermarket chain. The intent was to attract customers, who come in the store to purchase food, to buy the supermarket's own branded products and services—including banking, mobile-phone, and credit-card services; home and car insurance; and even on-demand movie- and TV-streaming services. Customers are already in the buying mindset when they walk into a store, so saving money on everyday products and services sold by a trusted brand should be an easy decision to make.

---

304. http://www.fastcompany.com/56804/beauty-simplicity
305. http://www.forbes.com/sites/parmyolson/2013/01/03/among-the-hot-trends-for-ces-2013-cars-that-run-on-android/

Do whatever it takes to be better. If you can partner with or afford to buy a company that will help you grow faster at the right time to corner a market, then you should look at doing this before the competition does. Being first to market and gaining traction as well as a large proportion of the market share is what's important, so do whatever it takes to do this quickly. Be careful not to do anything out of line with your organization's values or make decisions that can be detrimental to your brand, though.

Final Thoughts

I hope you've had fun trying new ingredients and creating your own recipes for success. There are an infinite number of useful ingredients out there in the real world, just waiting to be discovered—I've brought together only a handful to get you started.

My final advice: be quick to apply what you learn from continuous trial and error. Doing this will not only build character, but also help you make the most of any insight you gain and become an expert so you can intuitively react to current and future challenges. Like raw ingredients needed to cook an amazing meal, early experimentation and expert advice are the necessary components for finding the best approaches for you and your team.

No matter where you are in your journey of self-discovery, exploration, and problem-solving, never give up. Continue taking the initiative, never settle for "OK," fix things that are obviously wrong, challenge the status quo, keep fine-tuning your ideas, and, I promise, before long you'll solve those really big tech problems.

Index

Kick Your Career up a Notch

Ready to blog or promote yourself for real? Time to refocus your personal priorities? We've got you covered.

Technical Blogging is the first book to specifically teach programmers, technical people, and technically-oriented entrepreneurs how to become successful bloggers. There is no magic to successful blogging; with this book you'll learn the techniques to attract and keep a large audience of loyal, regular readers and leverage this popularity to achieve your goals.

Antonio Cangiano
(288 pages) ISBN: 9781934356883. $33
http://pragprog.com/book/actb

You're already a great coder, but awesome coding chops aren't always enough to get you through your toughest projects. You need these 50+ nuggets of wisdom. Veteran programmers: reinvigorate your passion for developing web applications. New programmers: here's the guidance you need to get started. With this book, you'll think about your job in new and enlightened ways.

This title is also available as an audio book.

Ka Wai Cheung
(160 pages) ISBN: 9781934356791. $29
http://pragprog.com/book/kcdc

Make It Work

Do retrospectives the right way, and see how to get new ideas accepted.

See how to mine the experience of your software development team continually throughout the life of the project. The tools and recipes in this book will help you uncover and solve hidden (and not-so-hidden) problems with your technology, your methodology, and those difficult "people issues" on your team.

Esther Derby and Diana Larsen, Foreword by Ken Schwaber
(200 pages) ISBN: 9780977616640. $29.95
http://pragprog.com/book/dlret

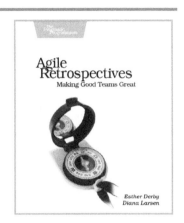

If you work with people, you need this book. Learn to read co-workers' and users' *patterns of resistance* and dismantle their objections. With these techniques and strategies you can master the art of evangelizing and help your organization adopt your solutions.

Terrence Ryan
(146 pages) ISBN: 9781934356609. $32.95
http://pragprog.com/book/trevan

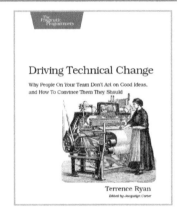

Redesign Your Career

Ready to kick your career up to the next level? Time to rewire your brain and then reinvigorate your job itself.

Software development happens in your head. Not in an editor, IDE, or design tool. You're well educated on how to work with software and hardware, but what about *wetware*—our own brains? Learning new skills and new technology is critical to your career, and it's all in your head.

In this book by Andy Hunt, you'll learn how our brains are wired, and how to take advantage of your brain's architecture. You'll learn new tricks and tips to learn more, faster, and retain more of what you learn.

You need a pragmatic approach to thinking and learning. You need to *Refactor Your Wetware.*

Andy Hunt
(288 pages) ISBN: 9781934356050. $34.95
http://pragprog.com/book/ahptl

This book is about creating a remarkable career in software development. In most cases, remarkable careers don't come by chance. They require thought, intention, action, and a willingness to change course when you've made mistakes. Most of us have been stumbling around letting our careers take us where they may. It's time to take control. This revised and updated second edition lays out a strategy for planning and creating a radically successful life in software development.

Chad Fowler
(232 pages) ISBN: 9781934356340. $23.95
http://pragprog.com/book/cfcar2

Be Agile

Don't just "do" agile; you want to *be* agile. We'll show you how.

The best agile book isn't a book: *Agile in a Flash* is a unique deck of index cards that fit neatly in your pocket. You can tape them to the wall. Spread them out on your project table. Get stains on them over lunch. These cards are meant to be used, not just read.

Jeff Langr and Tim Ottinger
(110 pages) ISBN: 9781934356715. $15
http://pragprog.com/book/olag

Here are three simple truths about software development:

1. You can't gather all the requirements up front. 2. The requirements you do gather will change. 3. There is always more to do than time and money will allow.

Those are the facts of life. But you can deal with those facts (and more) by becoming a fierce software-delivery professional, capable of dispatching the most dire of software projects and the toughest delivery schedules with ease and grace.

Jonathan Rasmusson
(280 pages) ISBN: 9781934356586. $34.95
http://pragprog.com/book/jtrap

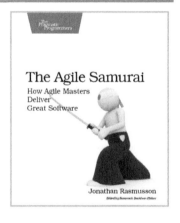

The Joy of Math and Programming

Rediscover the joy and fascinating weirdness of pure mathematics, or get your kids started programming in JavaScript.

Mathematics is beautiful—and it can be fun and exciting as well as practical. *Good Math* is your guide to some of the most intriguing topics from two thousand years of mathematics: from Egyptian fractions to Turing machines; from the real meaning of numbers to proof trees, group symmetry, and mechanical computation. If you've ever wondered what lay beyond the proofs you struggled to complete in high school geometry, or what limits the capabilities of the computer on your desk, this is the book for you.

Good Math
A Geek's Guide to the Beauty of Numbers, Logic, and Computation

Mark C. Chu-Carroll
Edited by John Osborn

Mark C. Chu-Carroll
(250 pages) ISBN: 9781937785338. $34
http://pragprog.com/book/mcmath

You know what's even better than playing games? Creating your own. Even if you're an absolute beginner, this book will teach you how to make your own online games with interactive examples. You'll learn programming using nothing more than a browser, and see cool, 3D results as you type. You'll learn real-world programming skills in a real programming language: JavaScript, the language of the web. You'll be amazed at what you can do as you build interactive worlds and fun games.

3D Game Programming for Kids
Create Interactive Worlds With JavaScript

Chris Strom
Edited by Fahmida Y. Rashid

Chris Strom
(250 pages) ISBN: 9781937785444. $36
http://pragprog.com/book/csjava

Seven Databases,
Seven Languages

There's so much new to learn with the latest crop of NoSQL databases. And instead of learning a language a year, how about seven?

Data is getting bigger and more complex by the day, and so are your choices in handling it. From traditional RDBMS to newer NoSQL approaches, *Seven Databases in Seven Weeks* takes you on a tour of some of the hottest open source databases today. In the tradition of Bruce A. Tate's *Seven Languages in Seven Weeks*, this book goes beyond your basic tutorial to explore the essential concepts at the core of each technology.

Eric Redmond and Jim R. Wilson
(354 pages) ISBN: 9781934356920. $35
http://pragprog.com/book/rwdata

You should learn a programming language every year, as recommended by *The Pragmatic Programmer*. But if one per year is good, how about *Seven Languages in Seven Weeks*? In this book you'll get a hands-on tour of Clojure, Haskell, Io, Prolog, Scala, Erlang, and Ruby. Whether or not your favorite language is on that list, you'll broaden your perspective of programming by examining these languages side-by-side. You'll learn something new from each, and best of all, you'll learn how to learn a language quickly.

Bruce A. Tate
(330 pages) ISBN: 9781934356593. $34.95
http://pragprog.com/book/btlang

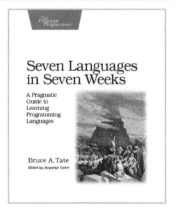

The Pragmatic Bookshelf

The Pragmatic Bookshelf features books written by developers for developers. The titles continue the well-known Pragmatic Programmer style and continue to garner awards and rave reviews. As development gets more and more difficult, the Pragmatic Programmers will be there with more titles and products to help you stay on top of your game.

Visit Us Online

This Book's Home Page
http://pragprog.com/book/ec101di
Source code from this book, errata, and other resources. Come give us feedback, too!

Register for Updates
http://pragprog.com/updates
Be notified when updates and new books become available.

Join the Community
http://pragprog.com/community
Read our weblogs, join our online discussions, participate in our mailing list, interact with our wiki, and benefit from the experience of other Pragmatic Programmers.

New and Noteworthy
http://pragprog.com/news
Check out the latest pragmatic developments, new titles and other offerings.

Save on the eBook

Save on the eBook versions of this title. Owning the paper version of this book entitles you to purchase the electronic versions at a terrific discount.

PDFs are great for carrying around on your laptop—they are hyperlinked, have color, and are fully searchable. Most titles are also available for the iPhone and iPod touch, Amazon Kindle, and other popular e-book readers.

Buy now at *http://pragprog.com/coupon*

Contact Us

Online Orders:	*http://pragprog.com/catalog*
Customer Service:	*support@pragprog.com*
International Rights:	*translations@pragprog.com*
Academic Use:	*academic@pragprog.com*
Write for Us:	*http://pragprog.com/write-for-us*
Or Call:	+1 800-699-7764

CPSIA information can be obtained at www.ICGtesting.com
Printed in the USA
LVOW02s1625261113

362912LV00011B/34/P